Feminism and Politics

Feminism and Politics

A Comparative Perspective

Joyce Gelb

UNIVERSITY OF CALIFORNIA PRESS

BERKELEY LOS ANGELES LONDON

University of California Press
Berkeley and Los Angeles, California

University of California Press, Ltd.
London, England

LIBRARY OF CONGRESS
Library of Congress Cataloging-in-Publication Data

Gelb, Joyce, 1940–
    Feminism and politics: a comparative perspective / Joyce Gelb.
        p. cm.
    Bibliography: p.
    Includes index.
    ISBN 0-520-06307-4 (alk. paper)
    1. Women in politics—Cross-cultural studies. 2. Women's rights—
Cross-cultural studies. 3. Feminism—Cross-cultural studies. I. Title.
HQ1236.G45   1989
305.4'2—dc19   88-10773
                                                                          CIP

Printed in the United States of America
1   2   3   4   5   6   7   8   9

For Andrew, Joe, and Jonathan

Contents

Preface

Two experiences inspired me to write this book. The first was research undertaken for a book on women and public policies in the United States during the years 1976–80. The second was a visit to the United Kingdom in 1980 during a sabbatical semester. At that time I became fascinated by the very different direction the British feminist movement seemed to have taken, and I wanted to learn why the divergent British structures and values had emerged. Over the next six years I visited England for research three times; and on a separate trip I also visited Sweden, a nation noted for progressive egalitarian policies. Meanwhile I continued to follow events and interview principals in the American women's movement. It is my hope that the unique contribution of this book is to provide a comparative political framework for analysis of the context and evolution of feminist movements, thus augmenting the fine work that has been done by other scholars who have studied disparate aspects of feminist politics in various nations.

The list of people and organizations to whom I owe a debt of thanks for helping to make this research possible is almost too long to record. I am particularly grateful to those who provided financial support for the project.

Significant among these was the Fulbright Commission, which provided me with a three-month grant-in-aid to the United Kingdom in 1982. This opportunity to conduct interviews and undertake firsthand research, with the kind cooperation of the Institute of Education at the University of London (thanks to the gracious invitation of a colleague, Margherita Rendel), proved absolutely crucial. Additional financial support for overseas research was made available by the Faculty Senate of the City College of New York and the financial office of the Graduate Center of the City University of New York.

I would also like to thank the Henry A. Murray Research Center at Radcliffe College of Harvard University, where I spent part of the fall semester of 1985. The opportunity to share my ideas with other visiting scholars and the staff was invaluable and helped sharpen much of my thinking. I owe particular thanks to the Rockefeller Foundation for providing me with the wonderful opportunity to spend an idyllic and highly productive month at the Villa Serbelloni in Bellagio, Italy, in the fall of 1985. The beautiful surroundings, unlimited time to work uninterruptedly, and stimulating colleagues provided me with a work experience that I shall never forget. My great appreciation is extended also to the Arbetslivcentrum in Stockholm, which generously gave me an office and research assistance during my stay in Sweden in May and June of 1986. I am grateful, too, for the help of the Swedish Institute, which arranged all my appointments in such an efficient and helpful fashion.

Good feedback and stimulating suggestions emerged when I had the opportunity to present excerpts from this book to the academic community—at Radcliffe, Columbia University, the Center for European Studies at

Harvard University, Augsberg College, the University of California at San Diego, and the University of Minnesota, as well as at a City College Women's Faculty seminar and a symposium sponsored by the Center for the Study of Women in Society at the Graduate Center of the City University of New York—and when I presented papers at American Political Science Association and International Political Science Association conventions.

In addition to thanking these institutions for their support and assistance (and of course the people who make them possible), some individuals deserve special thanks and deep affection. Annika Baude of the Arbetslivcentrum not only arranged my stay at the center but also provided me with wonderful housing and, even more importantly, her moral and intellectual support and expertise during my stay in Sweden. Barbara Hobson, then of the Murray Research Center, helped me to rethink many of my ideas and finally to arrange the trip to Sweden that proved to be so instructive. Ethel Klein of Columbia University helped analyze data and gave willingly of her time. Norman and Barbara Gelb provided unlimited hospitality on my several visits to London; Alice Kessler-Harris made my first trip to Britain memorable. John Mollenkopf of the Department of Political Science of the Graduate Center of the City University of New York and Maud Eduards and Diane Sainsbury of the Department of Political Science at the University of Stockholm have my heartfelt thanks for their efforts. Diane Sainsbury was especially helpful in providing data and many stimulating comments. Marna Feldt of the Swedish Information Service answered innumerable queries with unfailing good humor and expertise as did the staff of the British Information Service. The many individuals in the United States, Sweden, and the United Kingdom who gave unstintingly of their time in interviews and often afterwards must be recognized here as well. It has been a happy experience to learn that there is an international women's network, and I am proud to have been able to meet so many active and vital members of it.

An extraordinary debt is owed to my family. My husband, Joe, and two sons, Andrew and Jonathan Gelb, have lived with this research project since its inception. Andrew deserves special thanks for help to a computer novice. They have lovingly borne my absences from the family and cheerfully accepted the long hours necessary to complete the project (they have also, happily, occasionally reaped the benefit of cross-cultural research by accompanying me on the travels the research entailed). An essential word of gratitude goes to my two typists, Audre Procter and Chris Pritchard, whose patience and help were invaluable. Finally, my thanks to Naomi Schneider and Mary Lamprech of the University of California Press and to copy editor Liese Hofmann.

While only I bear responsibility for the research and analysis presented in this volume, I hope that the many individuals and institutions who helped to support it will not be disappointed.

List of Abbreviations

ACAS	Advisory Conciliation and Arbitration Service
AFSCME	American Federation of State, County, and Municipal Employees
ALRA	Abortion Law Reform Association
ASTMS	Association of Scientific, Technical, and Managerial Staff
CBI	Confederation of British Industries
CLPD	Campaign for Labour Party Democracy
CLUW	Coalition of Labor Union Women
CND	Campaign for Nuclear Disarmament
CPAG	Child Poverty Action Group
DHSS	Department of Health and Social Services
EEC	European Economic Community
EEOC	Equal Employment Opportunity Commission
EOC	Equal Opportunities Commission
EPA	Equal Pay Act
ERA	Equal Rights Amendment
GLC	Greater London Council
GMWU	General and Municipal Workers Union

ILGWU	International Ladies Garment Workers Union
JÄMFO	Delegation for Research on Equality Between Men and Women
JämO	Equal Opportunity Ombudsman
LO	Landsorganisationen Sverige (Swedish Trade Union Confederation)
MSC	Manpower Services Commission
NAC	National Abortion Campaign
NALGO	National and Local Government Officers' Association
NARAL	National Abortion Rights Action League
NCADV	National Coalition Against Domestic Violence
NCCL	National Council for Civil Liberties
NCW	National Council of Women
NEA	National Education Association
NEC	National Executive Committee
NHS	National Health Service
NOW	National Organization for Women
NUPE	National Union of Public Employees
NWAF	National Women's Aid Federation
NWPC	National Women's Political Caucus
ODV	Office of Domestic Violence
OFCCP	Office of Federal Contract Compliance Programs
PAC	Political Action Committee
ROW	Rights of Women
SACO/SR	Swedish Confederation of Professional Organizations

SAF	Swedish Employers Confederation
SDA	Sex Discrimination Act
SDP	Social Democratic Party
SEIU	Service Employees International Union
SPUC	Society for the Unborn Child
SSKF	National Federation of Social Democratic Women
TASS	Technical and Supervisory Section [of the engineers' union]
TCO	Central Organization of Salaried Employees
TG	Townswomen's Guilds
TGWU	Transport and General Workers Union
TUC	Trades Union Congress
VPK	Left Party Communists
WAC	Women's Action Committee
WAG	Women's Action Group
WCF	Women's Campaign Fund
WEAL	Women's Equity Action League
WI	Women's Institutes
WNC	Women's National Commission
WOW	Wider Opportunities for Women
WRRC	Women's Research and Resources Committee
WTUL	Women's Trade Union League

1

Introduction

The 1960s and 1970s saw the resurgence of feminism as a social movement in virtually every Western nation. In each, the movement adapted to the history, culture, and politics of the society (Bouchier 1984). This book focuses on how cultural traits and political institutions have shaped feminist movements in Britain, the United States, and Sweden. As Helga Hernes (1983:33) has pointed out, women in the state occupy similar roles regardless of national boundaries: they are citizens, consumers, clients, and employees. But they are also claimants in the arena of public policy, seeking to gain economic and political rewards and contesting for power and access. This study examines the mechanisms and impact of their role as political claimants helping to identify and influence policies that affect their lives as women.

The purpose of this inquiry is to demonstrate how differences in British, American, and Swedish feminism relate to systemic and cultural differences. A major hypothesis of this analysis is that such differences, in the respective "political opportunity structures" (that is, institutions, alignments, and ideology), have patterned the development, goals, and values of feminist activists in each nation. In turn, it will be argued, movement structure and systemic differences have affected and constrained opportunities for movement impact within each nation. While the feminist activists in the United States, the United Kingdom, and Sweden share many objectives, they differ significantly in their style of political activism, leadership orientation, and organizational values (Jenson 1983). These differences interact with contrasting political opportunities to shape the success of feminist claims. The analysis defines alternate meanings for the concept of movement success. How the role of women activists themselves shapes political alternatives is a central question of this study.

Other political scientists have questioned the view that autonomous women's groups organized to fight for political power and policy gains are more likely to succeed than groups integrated into prevailing institutions (Adams and Winston 1980). This study will argue, based on the British and American experience and with a briefer look at Sweden, that gender-based women's groups that are separate from institutionalized interests such as parties and unions are more likely to develop independent strategies and political agendas of their own choosing, thus permitting greater political impact. This analysis seeks to demonstrate that autonomous feminist movements play a major role in the achievement of significant social change. Otherwise, women are acted upon as objects of social policy but are not participants in their own destinies (Siim 1982:34).

The three countries studied here were selected because they are all postindustrial Western democracies, with policies that are superficially similar regarding women's rights. Each has legislation on abortion rights and labor force equality (Sweden was the last to adopt the latter), and each has set up an administrative commission on equal opportunities to monitor sex discrimination laws, albeit with very different powers. Although all three societies have experienced similar trends, their significance for feminist politics differs. For example, while in all three nations women have simultaneously been mobilized and incorporated as new participants into the political process and into the expanding tasks of the modern state, particularly as these relate to women, these developments have proceeded in different ways and with different impacts in each nation (Hernes 1982:7).

The participation of women in the labor force has increased dramatically in each society, as have family "pathologies," such as divorce and female-headed families (although these are not viewed as "pathologies" in Sweden). Paradoxically, Sweden, which is noted worldwide for the equality in its progressive social policies, has the highest level of sex segregation in the labor force as well as the highest percentage of part-time workers who are women. In all three societies women and men are concentrated in specific occupations. Women are further segregated into a far smaller number of occupations than are men. These occupations are lower-paying; many are in the public sector service area. In one study (Jonung 1984:54) an index of sex-based dissimilarity in employment reveals 70.7 for Sweden (282 occupations), 66.1 for Britain (223 occupations), and 65.1 for the United States (441 occupations).* Another study has found Swe-

* The index is calculated as the absolute sum of the differences between the proportion of women in a certain occupation and the proportion of men in that occupation. The sum is divided by two and multiplied by 100. A score of zero indicates no segregation.

den to have a score of 60 percent, the United States 46.8 percent, and Britain 31.1 percent (apparently reflecting at least in part the fact that British men are less concentrated in a few occupations) (ibid.).

This study will focus on 1) the sociopolitical context in which each movement operates, 2) the organization and strategies utilized by each movement, and 3) the impact of each movement on the political process, public attitudes, and public policy. Within the context suggested, the study examines three Western countries that provide three different political models and therefore three different approaches to feminist politics.

To analyze the impact of women's movements on the political process and in helping to structure policy alternatives and outcomes, we will contrast three different models of women's participation and activism: 1) interest group feminism in the United States; 2) left-wing/ideological feminism in the United Kingdom; and 3) state equality in Sweden.

Interest group feminism is characterized by a relatively open political system, a focus on equal rights and legal equality (although many demands may go beyond mere reformism), and the creation of lobbying groups that may have a mass membership or be staff dominated. Networking and inclusiveness typify the approach to different political orientations within the women's movement.

Ideological, or left-wing, feminism is characterized by insistence on ideological purity and a reluctance to work with groups espousing different viewpoints. This type of feminist politics is decentralized and locally based, largely lacking a national political presence and impact. Fragmentation as well as enthusiastic commitment to sectarian (feminist) views typify this model.

State equality is characterized by the absence of a visible and influential feminist movement. Instead, women are active via political parties and, to a lesser degree, trade unions (as is true to some extent in left-wing feminism, as an alternative to local political action). The state has tended to anticipate or co-opt women's concerns into public policy, even without significant pressure from women's groups. Policies related to women are generally discussed within the framework of "equality" or "family" policy.

In this analysis, movement development, effectiveness, and impact are seen as largely dependent on external factors such as political environment and available resources. Among the environmental variables that appear to be particularly significant are the current political complexion of government, the structure of the central administrative process, and the state of the economy (Whitely and Winyard 1983: 10–11). Examination of the structure of British politics, economics, and social life suggests a society highly traditional in its structure and values, a stagnant economy, and a centralized, secretive, and bureaucratically dominated system. These factors contribute to a political setting in which feminists tend to be isolated from the formal political system, from feminists with different perspectives and women in general, and from potential allies. Ideological divisions, rooted in class and other conflicts, inhibit the formation of coalitions dedicated to resolving women's political and economic needs.

We focus on the role and structure of feminism in the nations studied by examining two wings of feminism. The first is the women's liberation movement, often characterized as the more radical, or "younger," branch of the movement. Such groups in both the United States and Britain are distinguished by their emphasis on life-style change, provision of alternative services, and decentralization and anti-elitist values (Stacey and Price 1980:180). The second wing of feminism is that segment of the movement operating within the traditional policy-making structure. In the case of Britain, this segment participates in parties and unions that play a dominant role in the political system. In the United States, women tend to be effective primarily as interest group activists, given the primacy of pressure groups in the American political arena (although we will examine the role of women in parties and unions for comparative purposes). These two sets of feminist activists are roughly analogous to what Freeman has called the "militant" and "reformist" branches of contemporary feminism, although many British feminists would decline the honor of inclusion in the reformist camp. In Sweden, there is only one manifest face of feminism: that represented by women in parties and unions; the minute feminist movement is almost subterranean in character and visibility.

Among this study's major assumptions regarding the distinctions between the American, British, and Swedish systems are the importance in the United Kingdom and Sweden of centralized government and Parliament (called the Riksdag in Sweden) and the primacy of the administrative process.

Crucial variables affecting movement emergence and activism are the degree of corporatism/political centralization and pluralism. Schmitter's (1984) well-known definition characterizes corporatism as interest representation in which constituent units are organized into a limited number of singular, noncompetitive, hierarchically ordered and functionally differentiated categories, recognized or licensed by the state and granted

Table 1.
Distinctions Between Pluralism and Corporatism

Characteristic	Pluralism	Corporatism
Group unity/discipline	Low	High
Independence (economic)	High	Low
Character of state access	Open	Closed
Exclusivity of group participation	Unlimited	Limited
Character of state authority	Dispersed	Concentrated/ centralized
Consistency of issue resolution	Inconsistent	Consistent (planning)

a deliberate representational monopoly within their respective categories. Pluralism, in contrast, characterizes a society in which multiple, voluntary, competitive self-determined groups have access to state power. Table 1 makes the distinctions between the two approaches clearer. The United States, where strong or strongly structured pluralism prevails, is found on the pluralist/dispersed side of the continuum, while Britain and Sweden are placed close to the corporatist/centralist side.

In Table 2 we show how this structure may be supplemented to account for the organizational role of women's groups in the three nations studied.

The administrative process in the United Kingdom emphasizes ministerial responsibility and neutrality and operates behind closed doors, whereas in the United States there is far greater possibility for public scrutiny and intervention. British courts play a much more restricted role than their American counterparts. The American party system is looser and less dominant in the political system; and because power is fragmented—

Table 2.
Structure and Potential Role of Women's Groups

Structure	Sweden	U.K.	U.S.
Strong labor unions	+ +	+	−
Strong political parties	+ +	+	−
Strong promotional interest groups (change-oriented)	−	−	+ +
Women's section in parties/unions	+ +	+	−
Independent women's liberation group	−	+ +	+
Pluralist system	−	−	+ +
Politicized bureaucracy	+	−	+ +

NOTE: − = limited; + = important; + + = very important

both in executive/legislative relations and in the federal structure—it is more accessible to interest groups of all types. Swedish politics is usually characterized as a "consensual democracy" in which conflict and confrontation are customarily assiduously avoided. It resembles the British model of executive dominance and corporatism, although the political process incorporates a greater variety of groups.

The scope of government differs as well. In the United Kingdom the role of national government intervention in family and welfare policies (for example, the National Health Service) has been more firmly institutionalized, providing some support for British women in areas their American counterparts lack. Examples are child benefits (which are paid to mothers and were formerly called child tax allowances), maternity grants, and maternity allowances.

Welfare state benefits for women and children are greater in the United Kingdom than in the United States, including the non-means-tested child benefit of £5.25

per week, supplementary benefits, family income supplements, and rent rebates, although they are still far lower than those provided in most of the rest of industrialized Europe (the equivalent of $50 in British sterling, compared, for instance, with $93 in Hungary and $218 in France) (Norris 1984:43; Lewis 1985). After 1983, owing to a directive from the European Economic Community (EEC), married women on unemployment and sickness benefit could claim extra allowances for their children, although the new rights to Family Income Supplement and other benefits were significantly qualified by stringent requirements.

The United Kingdom has lower pay benefits for maternity and stricter eligibility conditions than any other European country (Dex and Shaw 1986:5; Coote and Campbell 1987:90–91). In comparison with the United States, Britain has legislated more extensive maternity benefits, but many women do not meet the benefit conditions. In the United States nearly half of women employees are provided with paid or unpaid maternity leave—large corporations are most likely to provide such benefits (Dex and Shaw 1986:14; Kamerman, Kahn, and Kingston:1983). Thus, despite the existence of statutory maternity benefits in Britain, more American women appear to get such support (albeit from the private sector) because there are fewer restrictions in the United States (Dex and Shaw 1986:14).

The British have the least day-care space available for children of working mothers (ibid.). American women are more likely to depend on paid and out-of-home child care than are their British sisters. British families tend to rely on family-based child care provided by husbands and grandmothers; few utilize institutional or nonfamily care (*Employment Gazette,* May 1984:209).

In the United States, antipathy to centralized state

power and reluctance to intervene in the family have resulted in a system of categorical grants; policies are fragmented and lack coordination, providing means-tested support only for poor women who are (mainly) single parents. The United States is alone among these three nations (and the democratic West as a whole) in having no national insurance system for childbirth medical expenses, no children's allowances, and no statutory care benefits to cover pregnancy and childbirth. Civil/welfare rights activities in the 1960s did, however, expand the public sector's support of the poor.

In Sweden, a generous policy of support is available to parents (of either sex) for child care, housing, and other benefits to ease the burdens for working family members. In 1971, child allowances were $212 in Sweden, $62 in the United Kingdom, and $0 in the United States; the ratio has not changed much since then (Heidenheimer, Heclo, and Adams 1983:207). The Swedes have sought to develop social programs with a view to labor force and market control; the British have tried to universalize social benefits but at a low level; the Americans have kept state intervention to a minimum. While the Swedish welfare state has sought to develop a minimum level of well-being for each citizen, the United States, via the "residual welfare" model, prefers reliance on the private market and family to meet individual needs.

In the United States, universal social welfare is not seen as a desirable social good; instead, the society provides remedial solutions to politically identified social problems (Boneparth 1984:45; Hagtvet and Buding 1986:291). The concern of American policy is for the family as an institution but not for the individual member of the family (Boneparth 1984:46). Family policy often tends to be dealt with at the state, rather than the federal, level; resistance to federal public spending in recent years has reinforced this trend.

The institutionalization of the welfare state in Britain has to some degree altered the nature of the debate about such feminist issues as abortion, because of the presence of the National Health Service (NHS). Nonetheless, less than 50 percent of abortions are in fact performed by the NHS, a number that may be limited even further by cuts in the NHS under the Thatcher government (Greenwood and King 1981:180). And there is a great variation in the availability and cost of abortions throughout Britain. As in the United States, politics in recent years has been dominated by conservative interests who have sought to slash budgets and "reprivatize" numerous public sector functions, including those specifically related to women dependent on the state. Even in Sweden, concern over financing the extensive welfare state in an era of a shrinking economy has emerged as a significant political issue.

The emphasis to be placed here on externally caused distinctions among the feminist movements in the three nations should not obscure the many similarities, particularly in comparing the movements in the United States and Britain. Among these have been virtually simultaneous (parallel) historical developments, including the advent of the suffrage movement, the birth control movement, in which each country had a comparable leading figure—Stopes in the United Kingdom and Sanger in the United States (and Ottesen-Jensen in Sweden)—and the "renaissance" of feminism in the 1960s. In addition, the Seven Demands of the women's liberation movement in the United Kingdom (Feminist Anthology Collective 1981) are markedly similar to those advocated by the National Organization for Women (NOW) in the United States:

1. Equal pay.
2. Equal education and job opportunities.
3. Free contraception and abortion on demand.
4. Free 24-hour nurseries, under community control. (This demand, of course, goes further than the American one for day care.)
5. Legal and financial independence.
6. An end to discrimination against lesbians.
7. Freedom from intervention by the threat of violence or sexual coercion, regardless of marital status. An end to the laws, assumptions, and institutions that perpetuate male dominance and men's oppression of women.

It is significant that in Sweden a major statement, "Toward Equality," was adopted in 1969 by the dominant Social Democratic Party. Among its major and primarily economically oriented goals are a society in which "rights, obligations, and work are no longer allocated according to sex." This manifesto calls for equality in working life: eradication of sex discrimination in recruitment, promotion, and wages; economic independence for married partners, with the two-wage-earner family as a model; uniform taxes for all; and parental leave (Qvist, Acker, and Lorwin 1984:265–66).

Analysis of public policy reveals similar trends. In the area of equal rights, the United Kingdom passed an Equal Pay Act (1970) and Sex Discrimination Act (1975), the latter establishing an Equal Opportunities Commission (EOC) to enforce the new laws. The Employment Protection Act of 1975 gave women a statutory right to paid maternity leave, protection from unfair dismissal during pregnancy, and a guaranteed maternity leave of 29 weeks. (However, as will be discussed later, these policies have been made more restrictive by the Thatcher administration, which has institutionalized stringent requirements concerning prior work for would-be recipients [Coote and Campbell 1987:93–94.]) With regard to violence and victimization of women and the right to self-determination, the Domestic Violence and Matrimonial Proceedings Act (1976) strengthened procedures by which women could obtain injunctions to restrain violent husbands, while the Sexual Offenses (Amendment) Act of 1976 provided better safeguards for a rape victim's privacy during trial (ibid., 37, 42). The 1967 Abortion Act authorized abortion up to 28 weeks of pregnancy in cases where two doctors agreed either that the life of the mother or other children would be at risk or that the baby was likely to be handicapped (Randall 1982:172).

In the United States, Title VII of the Civil Rights Act of 1964 and the establishment of the Equal Employment Opportunity Commission (EEOC) provided equal employment protection for women. The 1978 Pregnancy Discrimination Act gave pregnant women equal access to insured maternity benefits.

Abortion rights in the United States were established largely via Supreme Court decisions (whereas in the United Kingdom they were enacted by legislation) and have been the subject of congressional action (primarily restrictive). Domestic-violence legislation (which involved funding for shelters, not procedural reform) was enacted in 1984 at the federal level, and additional funding for victims and shelter expansion, as well as improved police and judicial intervention, has been the subject of considerable legislative activity at the state level.

In Sweden, legislation permitting women to choose abortion freely up to the eighteenth week of pregnancy was passed in 1975 (although abortion after the twelfth week is subject to a special inquiry). After 1982, wife beating became open to public prosecution and, in March 1985, government grants were made available to aid some shelter activities. Equal opportunities legislation that prohibits sex-based discrimination in employment and requires employers to take steps to promote work equality was enacted into law in 1979. Despite the apparently similar nature of public policy related to women in the three nations, however, we will contend that the impact of such policy has depended in large measure on systemic factors and the strength of the organized feminist movement.

Social movements may be described as movements seeking to achieve social change through collective action. Directed groups (with more formal organizational structures) have formal leadership, definitive ideology, stated objectives, and specific programs. Nondirected movements stress a reshaping of perspectives and values through personal interaction (Hanmer 1977:92).

To a large extent, the most visible portion of the American feminist movement belongs to the "directed" category, at least in its formal leadership structure and definite programs of action. To a greater degree, British feminism is of a more "nondirected" nature, with greater emphasis on personal interaction, expression and articulation of feminist values, and the importance of internal democracy.

In addition, coalitional activities across issue and ideological lines are less well developed in the United Kingdom than in the United States. Hence, pressure group politics has not been the primary avenue for feminist involvement in Britain. However, the absence of formal, structured coalitional groups comparable to those in the United States should not obscure the existence of alternative groups actively involved in other aspects of political life.

As we have noted, in Sweden, feminist movement activity per se has been limited and women's organizations have tended to gravitate toward political parties. Some efforts to create all-party, gender-based groups have been made in recent years, and ad hoc activity has occurred around some women's issues (especially opposition to prostitution, pornography, and violence against women).

The Political Opportunity Structure

This analysis rests on the premise that political structures provide the context for the development of social movement politics. Analysis of political structures includes the assessment of the significance of parties, pressure groups, the bureaucracy, the nature of state power, and the role of the judiciary. In addition, processes of socioeconomic change, including values and issue approaches, must be considered. External factors help structure the type of group mobilization that occurs as well as the character and success of a movement. Because British politics operate within a neocorporatist framework, large, economically labor-related pressure groups are primary actors in politics, although they are less well integrated into regimes dominated by the Conservative Party. There appears to be little support for Samuel Beer's view that British pressure groups are strong when promotional groups are considered. Most students of British politics agree that the nonorganized and lesser-organized are rarely consulted by policymakers (Richardson and Jordan 1979:45). Gender, rather than economic sources of influence, is inevitably rendered less important in such a system.

Richardson and Jordan (ibid., 122) have characterized the British political system in terms of strategies for group influence; in their view, Whitehall is the primary target for influence; the legislative process comes second, and the public third. To a remarkable degree, the policy-making process is organized in an exclusive fashion (Ashford 1981:8). In fact, it may be suggested that the British political system tends to limit access for non-established, "promotional" groups, which seek social change. While producers—or key economic groups— may enjoy continued access to policy-making, based on sectional and economic roles and well-established relationships, the same is not true for groups, consumers, or others who may oppose them. A consequence of centralization and secrecy is to limit the role of "promotional" or attitude groups seeking change—they tend to be poor in size, finances, and the ability to obtain benefits (Christoph 1974:44; Blondel 1974).

Economic and technical problems are most often dealt with by a system that increasingly emphasizes executive dominance (Smith 1976:66–67). The role of Parliament is diminishing in comparison to the administrative sector. Whereas in the United States political power is diffused, in Britain it is highly centralized—in both the horizontal and the vertical structures of policy-making. (Grass-roots lobbying, common in the United States, has little impact in a system as centralized as that in Britain.) The administrative sector is characterized by limited public visibility and the absence of public scrutiny of decision-making (Pennock and Chapman

1969:11). The core of "politically neutral" permanent civil servants and the relatively small size and narrow social backgrounds of the political elite often present significant barriers to change-oriented policies (Ashford 1981; Sampson 1982). Cabinet meetings are secret, and closed doors are the rule in most administrative proceedings.

The system of "tripartism," which includes the government, the Confederation of British Industries (CBI), and unions, limits possibilities for other groups to influence politics (Beloff and Peele 1980:28). Pressure groups may present views but may have little impact on the legislative process or the cabinet (ibid., 238–39). Unlike the United States, where appointments to government, including administrative bodies, are often the product of "clientelism," or pressure group influence, in the United Kingdom such appointments are limited to "old boy" lists of the "Great and the Good." Confidentiality prevails, and there is virtually no opportunity for group activists to influence such processes. Traditional pressure group tactics are most successful for groups with high-level political or civil service contacts. (Less conventional forms of political activity, especially protest, may endanger opportunities to relate to government) (Grant 1984:134). The absence of alternative methods of access to the political process virtually forces promotional groups out of the system. The secret process of nomination and appointment is made by the civil service in consultation with the prime minister and "leading mandarins" (Ashford 1981:266). Little is publicly known about patronage politics. Policies are established behind the scenes—knowledge is hidden from Parliament and the people. The highly stratified administrative system means that many crucial steps in the policy-making process are unknown to ministers, the public, and groups interested in specific policies (ibid., 19). Ashford has argued that because, traditionally, civil servants and politicians have not engaged in conflict, the political system has never confronted and subordinated the bureaucracy (ibid.). The feedback and friction generated by implementation politics in the United States are almost entirely absent in Britain, owing to the primacy of appointed, not elected, officials.

Although parties are, by general consensus, declining in importance, they are major agents for the resolution of key political issues. Because of the significance of strong parties within Parliament, legislation of a controversial nature must enjoy government (party) support or at least sufficient neutrality to ensure that a private member's bill is given the time to introduce and nurture legislation. The final stages of the legislative process are less important than the negotiations that precede them (Beloff and Peele 1980:107).

British parties, more than those in the United States, tend to be parties of social integration rather than individual representation. Party policy does not seem to reflect group influence to the extent common in the United States, with the possible exception of the relationship between trade unions and the Labour Party (Christoph 1974:13). In the Conservative Party, the parliamentary structure plays a key role, and the organization is less federal than in the Labour Party. In Britain, where about 50 percent of workers are unionized (in contrast to less than 20 percent in the United States), trade unions play a dominant political role, particularly in the Labour Party. Ninety percent of total Labour Party membership and 85 percent of the funds are derived from unions (Punnett 1980:127). The tradition of class-based ideology, socialism, and a strong organized left involves many British feminists in Labour Party and trade movement politics.

The passage of legislation is determined by the parliamentary timetable, individual M.P.'s, and the ruling party (Pym 1974:114). Pressure groups may create a climate in which reform is possible but cannot make progress against a hostile government; they cannot dictate a bill's content or guarantee its passage, although they may generate a climate for reform and raise public consciousness about a special issue (ibid., 120). The individual M.P. has little say in drafting or amending bills in parliamentary politics (Ashford 1981:17), so lobbying must have different goals than in the United States. The House of Commons creates or prevents a climate of opinion favorable to legislation proposed by the government (Richardson and Jordan 1979). In the legislature, because of the absence of permanent standing committees, interest group relationships with specialized legislators are less common than in the United States, although contacts with M.P.'s are more frequent than with civil servants. The absence of regularly scheduled elections serves as an additional brake on opportunities for political pressure.

In Britain the courts define themselves as defenders more of the state and the general interest than of individual rights (Nelkin and Pollak 1981: 52). The absence of distinct constitutional concepts and rules has limited the ability of courts to interpret (in contrast to applying) law. Judicial review in the American sense does not exist in the British system. Class action suits—such as those used to aid large groups in the United States—are limited or nonexistent. The system of administrative justice is a tangled web of appeals tribunals and admin-

istrative agencies with indirect and ambiguous relationships to the courts (Ashford 1981:40). Judicial recourse is limited by the role of industrial tribunals,
which hear most discrimination-related cases. There is
no general right of appeal from industrial tribunals.

New centers of power—including "quangos" such as
the EOC (to be discussed in chapter 4), which are largely
oriented toward achieving social goals—are autonomous
organizations, with advisory, executive, and policy-
making functions not unlike those of American regulatory agencies. Because they are not subject to parliamentary control, they have created new loci of power,
reducing the role of elected politicians even further (Beloff and Peele 1980:84). Quangos were initially viewed
as mechanisms for inadequately represented interests
to gain a voice in government in the postwar period, but
because of the systemic constraints outlined, they have
in fact been hard pressed to play such a role. Appointments to quangos are, as already noted, at the discretion of the ministers and civil service (Ashford 1981:39).

In Britain (and in the United States as well), local
government may sometimes provide greater opportunities for political participation than the national arena
(Beloff and Peele 1980:262) as there has been an increase in civic pressure-group activity concerned with
the quality of life and services.

As noted earlier, the American party system is looser
and less dominant in the political system, and the fragmented nature of power makes the system accessible to
a wider variety of pressure groups. Politics is less "corporatist"; unions are less socialistic and less politically
significant (Heclo 1974:18). Although in the United
States there is no analogy to the strong labor union role
linked to left and Labour Party politics in Britain, the

Democratic Party most resembles the Labour Party in its organization as a party of groups rather than of individuals (Freeman 1987). The past decade has seen the further decline of political parties and the rise of single-issue pressure politics. The American political culture stresses incremental, nonradical change as well as compromise. With the step-up of federal policy on social and economic concerns in the 1960s, the number of interest groups involved in lobbying at the national level increased greatly. Citizen groups, in particular, expanded their activities, prompted in part by the social unrest of the time, which provided a powerful impetus for change. New regulatory legislation provided a route into the political process for hitherto excluded and unorganized groups. Jack Walker (1983) has shown that citizen groups, including women's groups, were able to gain patrons in the form of members (contributors), foundations, other groups, and/or government, which enabled them to organize and then maintain themselves as political activists.

The American process of interest group activity was given additional momentum with the passage of legislation on campaign finance reform, which helped to further institutionalize group formation in the electoral process in the 1970s and thereafter. In the United States, in contrast to Britain, decision-making is subject to considerable public scrutiny, in both legislative and bureaucratic politics, partly owing to the dispersed process of decision-making not only at the federal level but also at other levels of politics. Students of American public policy have pointed to policy networks, or "subgovernments" (Heclo 1980), that permit specialists in Congress, in the relevant administrative sector, and in pressure group organizations to play a dominant role in policy-making. While policy networks in many areas have given way to broader and more open and penetrable "issue networks" in the 1980s, this development only accentuates the significance of interest group actors in U.S. policy-making (ibid., 102). Interplay between several sets of political actors, both governmental and nongovernmental, is without parallel in the United Kingdom, at least as far as noneconomic groups are concerned.

To sum up, American politics is responsive to interest group demands if they are seen as legitimate, whereas the British government pays less heed to noneconomic-oriented group demands. (The Swedish government, to be discussed later, promotes—and to a degree controls—interest groups sympathetic to policies that are primarily economically based.)

A further aspect of movement politics in the constitutional/cultural setting is the role of third-party, or support, groups that may facilitate political access and provide needed assistance. Relationships with other reform/change-oriented groups may foster political consciousness and alliances that provide resources, access, and legitimacy for new movements (Parkin 1968). In the United Kingdom, movements such as the Campaign for Nuclear Disarmament (CND) helped set the stage for change-oriented politics in the 1950s and 1960s. The CND was probably the first major group to aim its strategies at the public—instead of only at decisionmakers—and in this way was a model for feminists who followed. However, the CND lacked a formal bureaucratic structure and formal membership, and although it was a major political presence and leading force in the mobilization of political consciousness for women, it was unable to provide a continuing institutional base on which emerging feminists could rely. In the 1960s numerous other social reform and environmental groups—including those successful in promoting pro-abortion policy and legalization of homosexuality, and opposing capital punishment—emerged politically, as did groups of university students.

Like their American counterparts, traditional women's groups in the United Kingdom survived the doldrums of the '40s and '50s and continue to have a mass membership base, although it is declining (Rogers 1983; Stott 1978; Randall 1982). While they do not identify with women's liberation, they do support some feminist demands and efforts to achieve them. But such British women's organizations as the Women's Institutes (WI), Townswomen's Guilds (TG), and National Council of Women (NCW) by and large eschew relations with socialist and radical feminists. They have felt little in common with a women's liberation movement perceived by the media and general public as antimale. Hence, the links to civil rights and other movements that provided resources and access for feminists in the United States are weak in the United Kingdom (Costain 1982; Gelb and Palley 1987), although there are important ties to such groups as the National Council for Civil Liberties (NCCL) and the Child Poverty Action Group (CPAG), as well as a historic relationship to the socialist left, as we shall see.

In the United States, feminists were able to learn from the example of black civil rights groups and to rely on support from traditional women's groups. More recently, feminists have developed relations with a variety of political allies who have broadened their resource base and opportunities for access to the political system.

A final basis for contrast is the area of funding. Economic resources for promotional groups are scarce in the United Kingdom. In contrast, political scientists such as Jack Walker (1983) have stressed the crucial role played by patrons in the United States who contribute monetarily to both the formation and the maintenance of citizen-based promotional pressure groups, among them feminist groups.

In the United Kingdom, in contrast to the United States, there is relatively little money available for charitable gifts and little incentive for individual donors, who derive no direct financial benefit from contributions. Persons who wish to make annual payments to charities must sign a "covenant" for more than three years that obliges them to an annual payment (the charity receives the tax on earned income in lieu of the government; only individuals in the highest tax brackets are able to escape taxation up to £3,000). Apparently only a relatively few wealthy individuals are motivated to contribute in this manner. As in the United States, charitable status is not given to groups of a primarily "political" nature, although some campaigning is usually considered permissible by the Charities Commission. The limited nature of charitable income available in the United Kingdom is evident from a study revealing that 81 percent of charities have annual incomes of less than £500 (Phillips 1982). Of the small number of charitable trusts, few contribute to feminist groups. In the main, only government agencies such as the EOC and the Manpower Services Commission (MSC) have provided any funds for feminist-related activity. Although American feminists are among the poorest of recipient groups, the infrastructure of contributors in the United States from both private and public sources supplies far more resources to emergent groups and movements than is the case in the United Kingdom.

American feminists have been able to rely on continuing, and in some periods even expanding, contributions from members, wealthy individuals, and foundations. For example, contributions increased in the post-1980 Reagan election period after the Equal Rights Amendment (ERA) failed to be ratified. Contributions have enabled groups to survive, and in some instances even expand, despite a very real decline in federal government support in the 1980s (Peterson and Walker 1986:7), although the fortunes of membership groups depend in part on issue visibility and changing political orientations. At the same time, lacking formal membership and funding, British feminist groups have tended to remain small and less bureaucratic, and thus further isolated from the centers of decision-making power.

The Economic and Cultural Setting

In this analysis, economic and social factors, including values, attitudes toward change, and receptivity to new movements, are viewed as variables that influence the emergence and impact of new political claimants. Thus, they help provide the context in which movements such as feminism may emerge and flourish or, instead, fail to gain political strength and importance. Cultural differences, then, interact with political institutions and ideology to produce a climate in which opportunities for change are structured. In turn, the type of movement that develops and what we have called the "political opportunity structure" create systemic possibilities and/ or constraints that either promote or retard positive policy outcomes and political impact. The concept of political economy suggests the relationship between the state and the ways in which citizens pursue their private ends and satisfy their wants. In Robert Keohane's terms, if the rules of the game in a particular society allow or require actors in the economy to exert power over one another, then the "economy is political" (quoted in Levine 1986:5).

As noted earlier, British society is distinguished by its traditional structure and values. The British social structure, with its low educational attainment for women, norms of "good" motherhood and marriage, low wages, and a stratified labor market and class system, has greatly narrowed opportunities for political involvements (Hills 1981:13). The traditional family remains entrenched, to a degree unusual in Western society, with marriage rates high and divorce rates relatively low (Norris 1984:43). The rates for divorce continue to be lower in Britain than in the United States, although they have risen dramatically in recent years, as have the rates of out-of-wedlock births. The divorce rate is roughly half that in the United States (2.9 versus 5.3 per 1,000 persons). By 1987, 21 percent of live births were out-of-wedlock in the United Kingdom, in contrast with 20 percent in the United States and 45 percent in Sweden (Bianchi and Spahn 1986:74; Popenoe 1985–86; *Population Trends,* Winter 1987:52). The link between female-headed families and poverty is blatantly apparent from an analysis of the data. In the United States, 17 percent of white families and over 50 percent of black families were headed by women in 1984, an increase from 8 percent and 33 percent, respectively, in 1970 (Bergmann 1986:229). Black and Hispanic female-headed families were especially likely to live in poverty. Nonetheless, while there are fewer single-parent families headed by women in the United Kingdom, their numbers doubled between 1961 and 1981, and over 60 percent of Supplementary Benefit recipients are women

(Pierce 1980:84). Single parents received an extra £4.70 a week in Supplementary Benefits in 1987 (Social Welfare in Britain 1987:159).

Participation in the labor force by women, including married women with small children, has increased dramatically in Britain, the United States, and Sweden, as it has in virtually all Western countries. About 59 percent of British women are in the labor force, over 61 percent in the United States, and almost 80 percent in Sweden. Nonetheless, while in all three nations (and universally) women are concentrated in lower-paying, lower-status jobs, the situation in Britain appears to be worse than that in the United States and Sweden, at least partly because of Britain's serious economic recession, which has resulted in an even greater increase in unemployment for women than for men (although, as we shall see, the difference may be more apparent than real).

In the United States about 23 percent of women work part-time, limiting access to maternity leave, pensions, and job-training programs. In addition, part-time workers are usually first to be fired in cases of cutbacks and layoffs (UNESCO 1983). In Britain the part-time component (working 35 hours or less) of the labor force is especially large compared with that of other European nations (except Sweden) and the United States (Equality Ministry 1985:12). The most accurate assessment places the number of female part-time workers at about 42 percent in the United Kingdom, and rising steadily (the number is 46.2 percent in Sweden (International Labour Office Staff 1985:425, 459). Women often experience downward mobility when returning to work and are more likely to work at semiskilled or manual jobs. In 1982, 14.9 percent of British women were unemployed (in contrast with 9.4 percent in the United States [Edgell and Duke 1983:358] and about 4 percent in Sweden), although the unemployment figures for all countries appeared to be lower by the mid-1980s.

In the United Kingdom, several studies suggest that female unemployment is less than that of men because men have been disproportionately affected by the decline in manufacturing opportunities. (Thus, the statistics may reflect the ways in which unemployment data are gathered as much as actual statistical validity.) There was a perceptible narrowing of wage differentials between men and women during the 1970s when, perhaps in response to the passage of the Equal Pay Act (to be discussed in Chapter 4), women's gross hourly earnings increased from 63 to 74 percent of men's from 1970 to 1977 (Phillips 1983:15). Nonetheless, even these figures reflect hourly wage rates for full-time employees over the age of 21, so they considerably exaggerate the scope of the gains made (*Spare Rib*, Sept. 1979: 22). More recent evidence suggests a falling back to widened wage gaps based on gender (Coote and Campbell 1987: 18; *New York Times*, Jan. 16, 1984:B10).

The backwardness of the economy has further constrained opportunities and value change for women in the class-ridden, elitist British society, reinforcing the concept of the "family wage," which entrenches the leading economic role of male breadwinners and limits opportunities for women in the labor force (Land 1983). At present the contracting nature of public-sector employment and concomitant reduction in education and social welfare subsidies have reinforced these tendencies (Rothwell 1980:161).

Norms of political efficacy are unusually low in the United Kingdom, no doubt owing to difficulties of access in a centralized bureaucratic state, suggesting that political participation in general is likely to be limited (Barnes and Kaase 1979). Participation and efficacy are related to high income and educational attainment, both of which are especially lacking for most British women (only one-twentieth of them—in contrast with one-fifth of American women—have college degrees).

Although the women in all three societies analyzed here are more likely to be clients of the state and workers for it than power wielders within it, this chapter has sought to suggest that opportunities for the British feminist movement are constrained by the values inherent in a traditional society, a declining economy, and a highly centralized, closed political system. The next three chapters will explore the two wings of feminism by examining the structure of women's liberation and mainstream feminist activities in both Britain and the United States in order to develop a sense of how the "political opportunity structure" has affected movement strategy, style, and impact. We will then consider a different model, that posed by Sweden's "state equality," in which movement activism has tended to be absorbed by or incorporated in partisan and other institutions. In the concluding chapter, we will assess, within the comparative framework we have established, the meaning of movement "success" in each nation studied. Finally, we will evaluate autonomy versus integration as models for feminist aspirations.

2

Mobilizing Feminists:
Social Movements
and Political Activism

Social movements raise serious questions outside nor-
mal government channels, often concerning subjects
that are not being treated as topics of public concern
(Costain 1982:19). Such movements may be viewed
along a continuum from unconventional, almost spon-
taneous, sometimes illegal activity to movement groups
that seek more conventional political and legal change.
Social movement organizations are the acting compo-
nents of the movement, which may help turn grievances
into programs (Lowi 1971). It is the hypothesis of this
chapter that while American women's liberation groups
have moved closer to an accommodation both to the political system and to the more "reformist" wing of the
movement, largely because of an emphasis on coalition
politics and pragmatic achievements (goals), no such
tendencies are evident in the British movement. Rather,
there has been little institutional transformation since
the movement's inception in Britain, although constant
activity is maintained and proliferation and fragmenta-

tion occur owing to conflicts regarding strategies and ideology (Banks 1981:227).

Feminist theory about the role of women in politics and society may be analyzed in several ways. One is to differentiate between "reformist" and "radical" feminists. Reformist feminists seek equality through freedom—they do not seek to overturn the prevailing system, although they may be in conflict with those elements of it that they see as oppressive and hostile to women's self-determination. Thus, the stated goal of NOW is "to bring women into full participation into the mainstream of American society in a truly equal partnership with men" (Bunch 1981:191; Perrigo 1985: 129). In contrast, "radical" feminists perceive society as rooted in inequality, based on patriarchy, or male domination, and often on racism and capitalism as well. In this perspective, the only way to alter women's oppression is to transform the ideology and institutions of existing society (Bunch 1981:190). A somewhat different approach to the disparate views within feminism may be found in the distinction between "radical revolutionary" and "socialist" feminism. Socialist feminists, rooted more firmly within Marxist theory, insist on the primacy of the class struggle and seek to redefine those aspects of Marxism that seem inadequate to alter women's oppression to meet the needs of contemporary feminists. Socialist feminists wish to develop a strategy to jointly attack male domination and capitalism and thus restructure male-female relationships.

A second group, the "radical" (revolutionary) feminists see the source of societal inequality in the institution of male domination, or "patriarchy," usually rooted in biological differences and roles. Both the family and the state are seen to embody systematic male power and domination. In this view, alliances with men are not possible, since men are always oppressors and society cannot be reformed. Women must form "separatist" groups, shun relations with men, and seek an end to male domination (Randall 1982:5). Revolutionary feminists have forcefully restated many traditional radical feminist positions, especially hostility to men (*Spare Rib*, May 1979:82). Their major points of attack are marriage, the family, control of reproduction, and violence against women.

Although in both the United States and Britain elements of these different views exist, in the United Kingdom what we have referred to as "reformist" feminism occupies a far more limited role than in the United States. And, although socialist feminism exists in the United States, it has tended to remain outside the mainstream of the feminist movement, given the historic American antipathy to leftist politics. In turn, because British feminism is linked by reasons of history and ideology to the left and socialism, it has tended to develop more theoretical perspectives on the relationship between these two ideological tendencies. As liberal feminists Betty Freidan and Gloria Steinem have tended to dominate aspects of the American feminist movement, so have the socialist feminists Sheila Rowbotham and Juliet Mitchell been major forces within the British movement. However, two significant differences ought to be noted. First, the contributions of the latter two are less related to movement activism than to an interest in theoretical reinterpretation. Second, Rowbotham and Mitchell are not viewed as "spokeswomen" for or by the British movement, which does not recognize movement "stars" in any role at all. Radical feminism, sparked by such writers as Shulamith Firestone and Kate Millett, had its origins in the United States, although it has now gained considerable support among British women's liberationists.

For some observers, "revolutionary feminism" has eclipsed other significant strands within the British movement. An article in the *New Statesman* (Heron 1983) deplored the tendency toward "political lesbianism" in the United Kingdom, suggesting that many feminists had entered a social and sexual stage that denigrated engagement with existing structures that could lead to change. The author decried a new prescriptive definition of feminism that limited options and rendered the British movement no longer open to all women who recognized the oppression of women as a social group and sought change. Whether a new and more exclusive era in British feminism has truly dawned is difficult to determine; but such commentary does suggest a vast chasm between socialist and some radical feminists in the United Kingdom.

A final element within feminism is "cultural" feminism. It may be animated by either socialist or radical feminism, but its major concern is less political than it is personal: that is, it seeks to change life-styles and modes of behavior.

It is only a partial exaggeration to suggest that the American civil rights movement played a role in the creation of second-wave American feminism comparable to that of the socialist left in Britain.

Historical Background

The recent history of British and American feminist development reveals disparate organizational tendencies and styles. In the United States the New Left and the civil rights movement, each stressing different aspects of political equality, gave rise to the younger, or more "radical," branch of the feminist movement. As women activists in these protest movements became aware of their secondary status, based on gender, they began to develop new, female-based groupings. Early on, these groups stressed consciousness-raising as a technique to develop greater self- and group awareness and, like their British counterparts, created localized, participatory projects, including day care, rape crisis centers, shelters for battered women, bookstores, and self-help health clinics. A second group of feminist activists formed around the national and state commissions on the status of women. These commissions created a focus and forum for a different set of women, older and of a more professional and media-oriented bent, to begin to contemplate the need for a feminist pressure group. Their efforts were given additional impetus after the passage of the Civil Rights Act of 1964, which (almost by accident and certainly in the absence of any feminist pressure) was passed with the inclusion of Title VII, prohibiting sex discrimination in employment (Freeman 1975). The climate of expectations created by these two governmentally based actions, and the subsequent failure of the agency created by the Civil Rights Act, the EEOC, to enforce Title VII, led to the creation of NOW. Additional groups finally joined the Washington feminist lobby, including the Women's Equity Action League (WEAL), which initially rejected NOW's seemingly "radical" position on abortion rights; the National Women's Political Caucus (NWPC), focusing on recruiting and electing more women to political office and on legislative pressure; numerous groups concerned with single issues (abortion, health, education rights); and litigation groups.

The British Feminist Movement

The British suffrage movement early demonstrated tendencies that persist in British feminism today. One was an early link between the Labour Party and constitutional feminists (Evans 1977:126). Another was militancy—perhaps related to the example of Irish nationalism, perhaps born of rage and disappointment when apparently close-at-hand victory failed. Antisuffrage leaders and the Liberal Party served to isolate the movement and make it more sectarian and rigid (Evans 1977: 197–98). However, although suffragists were interested in engaging public power in order to gain the vote, contemporary feminist advocates in Britain are not so sure.

As in the United States, the contemporary British feminist movement received its impetus from radical and New Left politics, especially the CND and anti-Vietnam campaigns (Randall 1982:152; Wilson 1980: 184). In addition, working-class women in the 1960s organized as well: at Hull in 1968 for better conditions for their fishermen husbands and at Ford's auto machine works in Dagenham, where the demands for equal pay and equal work resulted in the creation of the short-lived Joint Action Committee for Women's Rights. This early effort at feminist militancy among working-class women seemed promising, but it has not proved as yet to be a significant element in British feminism, although in 1984–85 a new working-class women's movement, Women Against Pit Closures, emerged during the year-long strike by the National Union of Miners (NUM) (Wandor 1972:96–97; Coote and Campbell 1987:179–81).

The revived movement in the United States provided the immediate spark for much women's liberation activity, which early on developed strength among socialist and university women. A London-based women's liberation workshop coordinated over 70-odd local groups and published a journal, *Shrew* (Randall 1982:152; Wandor 1972:96–97). A national women's liberation movement held its first conference at Oxford in 1970. The demands that emerged from the conference—24-hour child care, equal pay and education, free contraception, and abortion on demand—reflected a practical orientation, new to some movement activists.

Like the "younger," more radical branch of the American movement, the British movement lacked a coordinating structure other than national, regional, or issue-oriented conferences. The British movement developed numerous factions; one chart listed at least 14 different "tendencies" within the movement (Sebestyen 1979:16). Conflicts within the movement—largely between radical and socialist feminists—have since 1978 prevented the holding of a national conference. The conflicts have centered largely on the scrapping of the six demands listed in Chapter 1 in favor of the seventh demand against male violence (Randall 1982:5). *Spare Rib*, a monthly journalistic publication produced by a feminist collective, and the London-based Women's Research and Resources Center (WRRC) today provide the only comprehensive foci relating to different elements within the movement. (A Women's Place, also in London, is similarly run by a collective of women and operates a bookshop and reference facility, as well as publishing a weekly newsletter.) The once significant Women's Information, Reference and Enquiry Service (WIRES) has been severely circumscribed.

Despite the absence of a focal point, feminist activities in the United Kingdom continue energetically. *Spare Rib* and other publications advertise a host of feminist activities, and numerous groups are listed under "Women's Liberation" in the London and regional phone books. However, unlike the mass-membership equal rights focus of the visible American movement, the major locus of activity is the small group, which, eschewing formal rules and leadership, prefers to arrive at decisions by consensus. The movement's character is also defined by the proliferation of small groups, each with a single-issue orientation. Even more "traditional" women's groups, such as Women in the Media and the National Housewives Register (founded in the early 1960s by liberal-minded housewives), operate on the basis of principles of participatory democracy and minimization of hierarchy and rigid structure (Stott 1981). It is possible that British women's experience with bureaucracy—in labor and leftist politics and, in the public sphere, in such areas as national health—has contributed to dislike of centralized, hierarchical power. However, though other British promotional groups began with a similarly diffuse structure, some, including the CPAG, have moved toward traditional interest-group organization. Often allied with feminist groups, the CPAG has developed a staff-dominated structure and a small membership as well, become more interested in fundraising, and sought to develop a parliamentary lobby. These activities are in marked contrast to the deliberately antihierarchical structure maintained by feminist groups (Seyd 1976).

Feminists have developed legal groups, such as Rights of Women, day nurseries, shelters for battered women, and pro-abortion groups. National coordinating structures have evolved to focus on specific issues such as abortion and domestic violence, but their scope is limited. Women's Aid was established in London in 1972 by Erin Pizzey to counter domestic violence and, somewhat unique in British feminist experience, was able to attract government and charitable funding (Coote and

Campbell 1987:141). Perhaps because it requires fewer resources than child care, domestic violence became a women's issue suitable for limited external support (Lovenduski 1986:79). The Women's Aid movement broke away from its founder on ideological grounds and has proliferated—with 99 groups and 200 refugees in 1980. Member organizations operate on feminist principles, with an emphasis on autonomy and self-determination for women (ibid., 42). Local women support the National Women's Aid Federation (NWAF) through adherence to its aims and attendance at meetings (interview, NWAF, 1982). Within the national and half-dozen regional offices, jobs rotate every two to three years to provide varied experiences for all and prevent domination by one person. Activists share in all work and there is no status distinction among the new staff members. Fund-raising is virtually nonexistent because of fear of creating strong central power, although resources from the national Department of Health and Social Services (DHSS) help pay staff salaries. While in the mid 1980s the London office of the NWAF was forced to close because of lack of funding, a newly modified collective structure has resumed national leadership in Bristol, England, as of 1988.

The NWAF's past activities helped create legislative reforms that gave increased protection to women against violent mates and imposed obligations on local authorities to rehouse victimized women. The NWAF also campaigned for more serious intervention by local police authorities (Perrigo 1985:135). (Women Against Rape, formed in 1976, has had some comparable success in raising consciousness and was in part responsible for the passage of the Sexual Offenses Act of 1976 making the rape victim's past sexual history irrelevant.)

A second organization that has developed a national structure is the National Abortion Campaign (NAC), launched in the spring of 1975 to defend the 1967 Abortion Act. It has a loosely organized mass base and operates from a socialist feminist perspective and on principles of participatory democracy (Marsh and Chambers 1981:1). The nonhierarchical, decentralized structure linking local groups claims a coalition of 400 organizations, with membership open to all who support its aims (interview, NAC, July 1982). In contrast to the operation of abortion rights groups in the United States, half the groups involved in NAC are trade union–related and receive some funding from the unions. Local groups are completely autonomous, deciding their own policy and method of campaigning. They have no elected officials or delegated structure. National policy is decided at the NAC annual conference and meetings are open to all members. An annual general meeting provides a forum for discussion of issues, although there is no mechanism for the resolution of conflicts on issues such as the role of racism and the broadening of the group's agenda to include types of reproductive freedom other than abortion. (In 1983, an organizational split between those who sought to focus on abortion as a single issue and advocates of broader reproductive rights divided NAC.) A national office provides backup resources and coordinates; a steering committee handles daily work. The staff is limited in policy-making authority, leaving most decision-making to annual and regional meetings. Volunteers are heavily relied on, particularly in the absence of funds to pay workers.

The contrast with most American pro-abortion groups is marked: U.S. organizations, such as the National Abortion Rights Action League (NARAL) and Planned Parenthood, tend to be professionalized, hierarchical in structure, and reliant on—although not necessarily directly responsible to—a dues-paying, mass-membership constituency. Such groups may fit the model of reliance on a "conscience constituency" in which contributors supply movement resources without direct material benefit. Effective policy-making is in the hands of the full-time staff, as in the "funded social movement organizations" described by McCarthy and Zald (1977). Abortion rights groups lobby extensively to prevent progressive weakening of abortion legislation and, in marked contrast to the British experience, where courts have virtually no role in this policy area, have been active in litigating to preserve and strengthen abortion rights. NAC's strategy is largely extraparliamentary, emphasizing proselytizing through demonstrations and picketing (Marsh and Chambers 1981:48), influencing Parliament by showing M.P.'s that grass-roots support for abortion rights exists.

In the United Kingdom, even groups with a national focus are ambivalent about campaigning (lobbying) and the legislative process, although in fact the NWAF and NAC have intervened effectively in the political system. In 1975, NAC mobilized 20,000 supporters to defeat James White's antiabortion bill. It has collaborated with other sections of the pro-abortion lobby, including the Abortion Law Reform Association (ALRA), and with Labour Party women. NAC supporters have been active in unions and have gained support from the Trades Union Congress (TUC) for their efforts (Perrigo 1985: 134). In July 1981, they held their first meeting with representatives from the trade union movement and Labour Party constituency parties in an effort to gain commitments for positive legislation on abortion. (After this meeting, a first attempt to enact legislation making abortion facilities mandatory under the NHS was introduced, and although it failed, it gained some media attention, perhaps setting the stage for further efforts [*Spare Rib*, Sept. 1981:106].) Because NAC's members are socialist feminists (drawn from the International Marxist Group), they have close ties to the Labour Party and trade union movement, particularly the National Union of Public Employees (NUPE) and the National and Local Government Officers' Association (NALGO) (Lovenduski 1986:80). The potential of this alliance was evident in 1979 when a mass demonstration (some 100,000 people showed up), with major participation by the TUC, helped stop the Corrie bill, which threatened to reduce access to legal abortions. This was the largest union demonstration ever held in Britain for a noneconomic issue, and it demonstrated the mobilization potential inherent in the feminist movement. However, at the NAC National Congress in September 1983, a split developed over the organization's need to cover other areas of women's reproductive rights, including contraception and sterilization. A new group, the Women's Reproductive Rights Group, was formed as a result of this disagreement, further contributing to the proliferation of women's liberation groups (Perrigo 1985:134).

A second effort related to women's liberation, though not strictly part of it, has been the mobilization of Greenham Common women in protest against a cruise missile installation in Britain. Organized around feminist principles, and exclusively populated by women (and children), it has numbered some 30,000 women in rotating order. Utilizing principles of nonviolence, even when arrested and subject to police harassment and eviction attempts, these women have helped mobilize national consciousness about peace issues based on feminist ideology.

Other feminist groups, such as Rights of Women (ROW), exist in the field of law and have been active for the past decade. Their goal has been to provide legal advice to the women's movement, formulate legal policy, and campaign on issues of concern to women. They have produced informational material, discussion documents, parliamentary briefings, and responses to government publications in areas such as violence against women, rights of lesbians, and family law. Nonetheless, the movement lacks a professional campaigning body of women lawyers, partly owing to funding problems (Williscroft 1985:100). Another promotional group, the NCCL, has had a women's officer active since 1975 and has played an important role in movement politics.

A movement comparable to the liberal feminist structure in the United States (to be described in the next section) does not really exist in the United Kingdom. Nonetheless, while never dominant in the British feminist movement (and likely never to be), there are groups that seek to play a centrist, coordinating role. Among these are the Fawcett Society (with roots in the suffrage movement) and Women in the Media. The Fawcett Society remains a small group of only about 375 members, its efforts to develop a membership base in northeast England having failed. Women in the Media, organized in 1970, has engaged in active campaigning for equal pay and for legislation against sex discrimination. Other groups that do not identify with women's liberation, but do support many feminist demands and efforts to achieve them, are current manifestations of more traditional women's activities. Among them are the WI, with a membership base of 400,000; the TG, with 217,000;

the British Federation of University Women, with 14,000; and the NCW, with 5,000 (Stott 1980). While these groups often support women's rights, by and large they eschew relationships with socialist and radical feminists.

Several new developments in Britain represent steps toward coalition building among different ideological groups in the women's community. In London in November 1980, a Women's Action Day involved some 67 organizations from a variety of women's perspectives and sought to discuss and develop common policies. A "women's agenda" was issued, dealing with issues of equal opportunity in law, education, work, politics, finances, the family, health, and the media. Groups represented included unions, NAC and ROW, traditional women's groups such as the NCW, and elements of the Liberal and Labour parties. With a grant from the EOC, the Women's Action Group (WAG) created a Lobby Pack with questions to be put to candidates for by-elections and parliamentary election (Pamela Robinson, Women in the Media, interview, Aug. 1982). Aided by funds from the Greater London Council (GLC), a number of feminist groups purchased a new building to share cooperatively in London. The EOC and NCCL have also provided opportunities for discussion of specific feminist issues through conferences and forums and helped link trade unionists with other feminist activities. The GLC Women's Committee and other local women's committees (to be discussed presently) have also sought to end centrifugal politics by involving a variety of women's groups as policy participants and recipients. In 1986 a campaign to defend children's benefits against restrictive cuts by the Thatcher government engendered a national effort. Included within the alliance, consisting of over 60 organizations, were the National Federation of Women's Institutes, Women's Aid Federation, Fawcett Society, and Mother's Union. The future significance of such cooperative efforts remains unclear.

A fairly new political advocacy group—the 300 Group—has sought to increase the number of women in the House of Commons (as of 1986 6 percent were women, up significantly from the previous election). Like its American counterpart, the NWPC, it aims to recruit and train women candidates for political office. It has sought to build a dues-paying base, in 1982 having a membership of 3,000 and dues of £12 annually (interview, Abdela, July 1982). Now under new leadership, the 300 Group has a central staff and offices, indicating its ability to endure and grow even though it continues to encounter hostility from traditional party groups that resent external intrusion and from feminists who dislike its relatively centralized entrepreneurial style. Nonetheless, it has trained well over 1,500 women and helped them gain an interest and confidence in politics.

The focus of most British feminist groups, however, is interaction emphasizing value and life-style changes. Consciousness-raising is an important element (though perhaps to a lesser degree than in the United States), and values such as self-confidence, skill attainment, and self-esteem are promoted (Randall 1982:164). The democratic character of the movement provides flexibility and permits accommodation of all types of grass-roots activity, incorporating diverse elements. As Mansbridge (1980:278–89) has pointed out, small size allows intense interaction, and continued face-to-face contact may prevent elitism. Yet, the group process, rather than attainment of group ends, may develop as a major focus (Freeman 1975:103–46). Conformity to the group may be encouraged. The absence of recordkeeping and repetition of old issues may retard group development (Adlam 1980:94). An ahistorical perspective may cause repetition of past mistakes. Decision-making may be slowed and the real administrative and political skills of some may be underutilized or ignored (Mansbridge 1980: 247). Individuals may become preoccupied with their own liberation and fail to seek more universal women's goals. And local, single-issue-oriented activity may reduce possibilities for national impact and comprehensive, as opposed to ad hoc, solutions to problems.

This analysis is consistent with Freeman's (1975:145) critique of movement structurelessness in the United States, in which she argues that the movement provided no coordinated or structured means of fitting local activity into other, existing projects. As she suggests, the consequence is that new groups form and dissolve at an accelerating rate, creating a great deal of consciousness and very little concerted action, failing to consolidate old gains while moving into new areas.

Finally, unaccountability to a constituency may create irresponsibility and unrealistic expectations. Inability to agree on goals and pool resources weakens opportunities for creation of alliances (Bouchier 1984: 123). If, as suggested here, the women's movement in Britain is a "deliberately dispersed collection of groups, campaigns and political tendencies with no single ideology," the absence of coalitional structures prevents organization around multiple issues in a continuing fashion (ibid., 128–29, 218–23). The politics of personal experience, inward-looking and seeking redemptive lifestyles, has often eclipsed the overtly "political." Women's liberation politics is fragmented, centered on single issues, and without networks in which different views may find expression and audience. The British emphasis on personal politics has often, though not always, resulted in reluctance to engage in the politics of the state (Barrett 1980:228, 245). Although feminist politics may serve as a model for other leftist groups in its emphasis on autonomy, flexibility, and democracy, the lack of a coordinating mechanism and national political presence presents a continuing challenge (Rowbotham 1979:90).

American Women's Liberation

The structure of grass-roots, radical feminism in the United States is similar to that in Britain. However, even within this wing of feminist politics, recent developments have suggested somewhat different tendencies. For example, in shelters for battered women and in rape crisis centers, which emphasize the feminist ideology discussed earlier, professionals have often combined with feminist influences to provide services, negotiate with bureaucracies, write funding proposals, and develop more enduring organizational structures (Schechter 1982:38–39). While conflicts over the importance of service, self-determination, and politics continue to exist, there can be little doubt that such elements as networking, lobbying, and emphasis on legal changes are more evident in the American movement. Activists have mobilized around state legislation and legal change— and have often been less reluctant to engage with political and bureaucratic forces and to seek legitimacy than is true for their British counterparts. Structures have been modified as specialization has created more hierarchical organizations, including staffs and boards (ibid., 94–95). Schechter concludes that the need for government support has forced activists to modify practices and informal procedures. In some instances, "modified collectives" have sought a compromise between external imperatives and feminist principles (ibid., 100). From local coalitions, statewide and then federal efforts have been generated. There has been willingness to engage political authorities at all levels in order to gain resources and reform legal procedures.

Coalitions reflect a variety of influences—including traditional groups (like the YWCA), professional and service providers, radical feminists, and equal rights feminists from groups such as NOW—and emphasize the sharing of resources, access, and skills (ibid., 113, 148). To aid battered women, a National Coalition against Domestic Violence (NCADV) was created, which lobbied for passage of a Domestic Violence Act, built a large network of contacts, sought to build a dues-paying membership base, and wrote proposals to raise money from the federal government and private foundations. The coalition continues to monitor relevant public policy, disseminate information to state and local groups, and seek to retain a nonhierarchical, multiracial approach (interview, Mary Morrison, NCADV, October 1982).

In contrast to the British experience, change-oriented feminists have often been able to rely on government "insiders" to put forward issues and build government support for movement concerns (Schechter 1982). Hence, leadership and structure, engagement with political forces at all levels, and the need for coalition have been treated differently in the United States than in the United Kingdom. But, as an instance of congruence, women's liberation groups in both countries have tended to focus on single issues and do not necessarily coalesce with other movement activists in multiple-issue alignments. However, while in the United States a grass-roots women's movement still exists, it is less visible than formerly and has to a greater degree joined forces with the more "middle-class" reformist sector of the original movement.

In the United States, then, though a grass-roots movement continues to exist, having successfully helped shape a new policy agenda based on the alternative services it created at the state and local levels, the character of the movement has changed considerably. In addition to the pull toward coalitions and political engagement we have described, to some degree overlapping memberships and joint activities have altered this segment of the movement's role. These linkages have been strengthened by campaigns to save abortion rights and pass the ERA, which have tended to unite feminists of all ideologies.

In addition, NOW, although founded as a feminist pressure group from the top down, has sought to move further in the direction of feminist principles than might earlier have been expected. First, it has sought (though not always successfully) to break down traditional organizational roles, combining staff and elected positions and thus creating a more participatory structural setting. Second, it has moved to adopt more controversial issue orientations, in addition to its continued interest in equal rights. The organization first endorsed abortion on demand, at that time (1970) and still a controversial political and moral issue. It also acknowledged, in an even more controversial act, that sexual self-determination—lesbianism—was a legitimate part of the women's movement. It has continued to examine alternative life-styles and support alternate forms of sexuality, even as it ages in political terms, indicating that it has hardly become more conservative with time. Finally, galvanized by growing evidence of the costs and consequences of the "feminization of poverty," NOW has joined with other feminist groups (who have come together in such events as the 1977 conference in Houston for the International Women's Year) and has moved to a more radical view of ways to eradicate poverty, although it clearly remains within the American (slightly left-of-center) tradition. And as the major feminist mass-membership group, NOW, though not always successful, has sometimes been able to act as an umbrella group for different interests within the feminist movement (Randall 1982: 235). As the most prominent feminist organization, NOW has to some degree eclipsed the more radical elements of the movement, because, given the American political system, its actions are more visible while its demands are viewed as both newsworthy and mildly radical. Though in many ways a traditional interest group, involved in electoral politics and campaign endorsements (to be described shortly), litigation, and lobbying, NOW's major significance for the movement continues to lie in its ability to focus public attention on key movement demands. It is able to do this through demonstrations, access to the media, and other social movement techniques.

But NOW does not operate alone in the political arena. Because the structure of American feminism has become specialized along issue and functional lines, groups such as NARAL in the area of abortion, WEAL on economic reform, and other organizations play a major role as well. In the area of domestic violence, the NCADV has become a leading voice. It may be argued that through the process, noted earlier, of coalition building and group mergers the movement has lost its radical edge and become limited by a turn toward more conventional politics. But the "legitimization" of American feminism as an interest group of political significance—at the same time as the movement has deepened its commitment to key feminist issues—suggests that considerable progress has been made from a feminist perspective.

The movement was strengthened by the creation of two types of women's groups: single-issue and multi-issue, or umbrella, groups. Single-issue groups dealing with abortion or domestic violence concentrate their resources and energy on one topic, keeping the issue before the public (Kolker 1983:212). Multi-issue organizations may have a broader range of contacts, a larger support base, and the ability to create coalitions.

NOW and other feminist-oriented groups gained additional membership and support from contributors, especially during 1980–82, in response to conservative threats symbolized by the Reagan election of 1980 and the defeat of the ERA in 1982. Membership in NOW increased to 250,000 in 1983 but had decreased to 156,000 by 1986 (Bomafede 1986:2178). During this period, in addition to strengthening relations with the more radical sector of the feminist movement, NOW built stronger links to traditional women's groups, including the League of Women Voters, American Association of University Women, General Federation of Women's Clubs, and National Federation of Business and Professional Women. Although some of these older, established women's groups had early on shared resources and opportunities for access with their feminist sisters, as the movement moved into its second decade, they too became constituents of feminist-sponsored, issue-based coalitions on key economic and other issues.

Finally, congressional and administrative staff members, primarily women, have played a key role in advancing women's issues. They help build support for feminist-sponsored policy, alert lobbyists about proposed, potentially negative changes, and provide the type of information only "insiders" can have (Kolker 1983:216).

While both in the United States and Britain a variety of theoretical and practical approaches to feminism constitute movement politics, in America the pressure to build coalitions and seek reform through more or less traditional interest-group politics has been notable. As we have suggested, networking across ideological lines is still rare in the United Kingdom, although it is a concept gaining support from many feminist activists. Traditional women's groups do have a mass constituency base in the United Kingdom (at least in comparison with other groups), but they are usually reluctant to join forces with those perceived, with reinforcement by media coverage, as being lesbian and antimale. The close relationship that has developed—in terms of resource sharing, political access, and even consensus on goals—between the so-called traditional women's groups and their reformist and radical feminist allies in the United States has no analogue in the political culture of Britain. The failure to seek advancement of women in existing political structures and the emphasis on sectarian politics have denied British feminists the mainstream voice their American sisters have been able to articulate (Weir and Wilson 1984; Coote and Campbell 1987:255). At the same time, the British movement has continued to be distinguished by its diversity and its capacity to celebrate difference and spontaneity.

3

The Role of Women
in Parties and Unions

As noted in Chapter 1, the resurgence of feminism in the latter half of this century has been characterized by the development of at least two wings of feminist organization. One wing, the autonomous feminists described in Chapter 2, has been more concerned with creating alternatives than with exerting political influence, particularly in Britain (Lovenduski 1986:63). The other wing has tended to emphasize rights and legal change and to operate within the decision-making process via traditional parties and unions or through a new set of lobbying-oriented interest groups. In this chapter, we explore two different approaches to legal and political change as manifested by British and American feminists, each constrained by the context of movement politics.

Parties: Britain

Despite the striking absence in British feminism of a counterpart to the dues-paying, mass-membership orientation of American feminism represented by such organizations as NOW, one may contend that in the British political system, such mass-based feminist groups are not necessary or even desirable. It may be argued that the functional equivalent of liberal feminism exists in Britain because, as suggested in Chapter 1, British feminists have historically been organized and influential as pressure groups within existing institutions, namely political parties and trade unions. Despite concern about co-optation and ideological dilution by male-dominated structures, feminists, especially on the left, have sought to develop alliances with these institutions to further their political goals. Nonetheless, this chapter suggests that increased activism by feminists has not ended a pattern of women's participation in these institutions that has been marked by "marginalization" and isolation from power. We thus share the view that existing political structures give little priority to feminists' interests; rather than seeking to solidify feminist strength and advancing women's interests, they have aided in their dissipation and fragmentation (Rasmussen 1983a, 1983b).

We will examine the role of women within party organizations in three ways: the role of women's groups within the parties, the role of women within the party hierarchy, and the party's approach to promoting women as candidates for political office. Underlying this chapter's perspective is the view that as Britain is becoming a more administrative state, the importance of feminist influence within groups whose major impact is on the legislative process may, in any case, be seriously debated.

Although women compose at least half the membership of the Labour and Conservative parties (Hills [1978] estimates a female membership of 40 percent in the former and over 50 percent in the latter), their role within party structures appears to be circumscribed. Women in parties and unions are organized into separate advisory groups having few powers and little ability to gain acceptance for resolutions they have passed. In addition, they are limited to reserved or set-aside seats on key decision-making bodies. In the main, the more significant a policy-making body is, the fewer women it has on it. Somewhat surprisingly, the Labour Party (founded in 1906), though closer to feminists on some policy issues and in ideological terms, has had no better a record on representation and power sharing than its Conservative opposition. Women are poorly represented within the party's annual conference (11 percent in 1980) and are allotted five seats of 29 on the party's National Executive Committee (NEC), the dominant administrative and policy-making body (Hills 1981: 17; Randall 1982:75). (Since 1960 only two women have been selected for the NEC by the constituency—or local—section of the party; none have been elected by the trade unions.) The principle of setting aside women's places on executive bodies is a well-established one in parties and unions, as we shall see. Because trade unions are dominant in the Labour Party and unions cast their vote in block fashion, in practice the set-aside women's seats are union controlled (Hills 1981). Hence, most women selected for the NEC are not independent feminists.

The Women's Section of the Labour Party is constituency based. Like other women's groups in similar institutions, it holds annual meetings and passes resolutions (interview, Gould, July 1982). Resolutions are forwarded to the NEC, which may or may not choose to consider them. (A National Labour Women's Advisory Committee acts as a liaison with the NEC.) In essence, then, the women's organization is powerless to affect policy and has no direct representation at the party's annual conference.

Unlike the Conservative Party, the Labour Party is a confederal organization, with a vast array of women's groups (as well as countless other political factions). In recent years, women's Labour groups have grown and proliferated—from the Women's Action Committee (WAC), associated with the far-left Campaign for Labour Party Democracy (CLPD), to a Women's Rights Study group established with M.P. Jo Richardson as chair. A group called Fightback for Women's Rights is active at the party's fringes. It has been especially vigorous in pressing for more channels to the Labour Party hierarchy—advocating that five resolutions be sent to the party's annual conference by the Women's Section and that women members be elected to the NEC directly by the Women's Conference. Fightback and WAC both espouse an end to all-male parliamentary shortlists (lists of candidates for final consideration). A Woman's Charter has been developed and promoted by WAC.

A measure of the expanded interest in women's activities was the upsurge in the number of women's delegates—from 320 in 1980 to 650 in 1981—at the annual Women's Conference. This increase indicated an intensified resolve to use the conference as a forum from which to articulate concerns and press demands on the party hierarchy. In recent years, there has been growing evidence of serious debate on key feminist issues (Perrigo 1985:142). At the 1982 party conference, party feminists sought to establish a more significant policy-making role. Their resolutions (thus far unheeded by the

party) called for the right both to elect the women members of the NEC directly and to send to the conference
five resolutions that would be automatically considered. Surprisingly, the Women's Conference defeated an
effort to make selection of women on candidate shortlists mandatory (Perrigo 1985:143; Vallance 1984:301).

The Labour Party hierarchy has responded to feminist pressure by appointing a national women's officer
and, more recently, designating a shadow minister for
women's affairs (with no counterpart in the present government), formerly M.P. Joan Lestor and now M.P. Jo
Richardson. A women's subcommittee of the NEC has
been created to formulate policy on women's issues. Its
members are also members of a National Women's Committee elected by women at regional conferences around
the country, thus providing a direct link between the
NEC and grass-roots women. A National Women's Charter drawn up by the NEC in 1982 calls for greater wom-
en's representation at all party levels and for day-care
services for women attending all party meetings (Perrigo 1985:143). Joyce Gould, the national women's officer, has sought to promote more female candidacies for
office. As of the mid-1980s, the NEC recommended,
though it did not mandate, at least one woman on each
shortlist. Constituency parties were permitted to establish women's sections without prior approval from the
party hierarchy (Coote and Campbell 1987:148).

The extent of feminist participation within the Labour Party is impressive and often channels socialist
feminist energy into party activities, but because of the
party's disarray at present, any victory may be a pyrrhic
one. In addition, there is some suspicion that several
groups seeking dominance within the party may be
using the feminist issue to build their own power base—
with little actual regard for feminist concerns.

And although the Labour Party committed itself (in its 1983 manifesto) to supporting abortion and contraception rights, measures against rape and wife battering, and equal pay for work of equal value, and to ending job segregation, promoting positive action, and strengthening the Sex Discrimination Act, it has yet to make these policies central campaign issues (Vallance 1984). Rather, as with women in general, such policies are isolated as women's issues and even treated as ethical matters on which M.P.'s need not be bound to party policy. Hence, it may be premature to contend that British women are emerging from a decade of isolation and an exclusive grass-roots focus to help unite the left and the Labour Party (Jenson 1982:343). In fact, though the party's feminist activity in recent years has expanded, it is not a new development. Nor is it clear that, at national-level party politics, major claims for feminist influence are supported by the evidence.

In the Conservative Party, women's participation in local politics is significant (perhaps 50 percent of constituency party chairs are women) but has not altered the pattern of "marginalization" we have suggested. While women are better represented at the party's annual conference (38 percent of the delegates were women in 1977–78), this body lacks the policy-making powers of its Labour Party counterpart (Randall 1982:74; Hills 1978:4, 8). Women constitute about 20 percent of the membership of the Executive Committee of the National Union, which is the highest point in the party hierarchy, although its policy-making and administrative powers are limited by the primacy of parliamentary leadership, consigning it to more of an advisory role. As of 1982, 50 of the 200 members were women, 19 of these being in statutory or mandated seats (European Union of Women 1982). At least one analyst (Hills 1978:6) has

contended that although Conservative women are better represented than their Labour sisters, they have only
limited impact at party conferences because they are
not very vocal.

As in the Labour Party, there is a women's national
advisory organization with its own annual conference,
now called the Conservative Women's National Committee. This committee often discusses women's issues
in the guise of such concerns as education (interview,
Hooper, July 1982). Another group affiliated with the
Conservative Party, the British section of the European
Union of Women, is active on behalf of women's issues
as well and was instrumental in stopping cuts in Social
Security proposed by the Thatcher government (Rogers
1983:34). This group has pressed for a party rule to include at least one woman candidate on shortlists and
for mandated interviews of women by candidate selection committees. It also recommended in 1982 that
women's groups within the party undertake candidate
education and training.

Prime Minister Margaret Thatcher's leading political
role in the party has not altered the position of women
in her party at all. She has consciously distanced herself
from women's interests and has neither appointed other
women to key positions (with the exception of Baroness
Young, who spent a brief time as Lord Privy Seal) nor
advanced policies of concern to women. (A vice chair,
Emma Nicholson, charged with encouraging more
women to join the party and Parliament, was appointed
after the 1979 election [Vallance 1984:302]). Although
Thatcher's campaign in 1979 stressed her image as a
housewife and mother, she has made it clear that she
does not view women's issues as a cause for concern
(Rogers 1983:171). (In 1986, however, Thatcher an-

nounced that women must be shortlisted for all public appointments and that an explanation must be provided for failure to comply [*Economist*, Nov. 1, 1986:53]). Thatcher has openly suggested that women with children should leave the labor force, and her government has steadily reduced nursery and child-care provisions, maternity and child-care benefits, and women's work rights (Rogers 1983:161). It is difficult to disagree with Richard Rose (1986:159), who has written that of the four women in the British cabinet from 1964 to 1969 (Thatcher, Barbara Castle, Judith Hart, and Shirley Williams), in no instance was their political stature derived from their sex or from their expression of feminist views. Both Thatcher's critics and supporters see her sex as largely irrelevant and her political views as significant. As the only woman in her cabinet, Margaret Thatcher demonstrates that high positions for women are an exception (Rose 1986:160). Nonetheless, Thatcher is assessed favorably for leadership qualities, for standing up for Britain, for ability to communicate, and for crisis management, suggesting that as a role model her position may augur well for future women in British politics (Butler and Kavanaugh 1984:296). However, as an indication that many women find Thatcher's policies wanting and may tend to reject them, the 1983 election saw a move toward the Alliance—the Social Democrat–Liberal partnership—and away from the major parties among women voters (ibid., 296; Rogers 1983:159).

Finally, with regard to candidates standing for election, women have continually been underrepresented in both major parties. They have also been consistently underselected by constituencies; even when they are chosen, they are selected disproportionately for unwinnable or marginal seats (Vallance 1984:304; Hills 1978).

Although in 1983, for the first time over 10 percent of the party's candidates were female, a third higher than in 1979, it has been argued that with regard to selection women are worse off today than they were a century ago (Rasmussen 1983b:309). As of 1983, only 3.5 percent of M.P.'s were women, in contrast to 5.1 percent of representatives in the U.S. Congress (Sainsbury 1985:4). By 1987, however, partially reflecting the effort by parties to reach out to women voters in a hard-fought campaign, over 6 percent of the M.P.'s selected were women.*

In the Labour Party the "A" list is union-dominated. In 1972, two of 100 candidates nominated were women; in 1977, three of 103 (Hills 1978); and in 1983, seven of 153 (or 4.5 percent) (Hills 1978; Vallance 1984:306). The TUC's increasing sympathy for women's concerns (to be discussed later) may aid in the future expansion of women's role in the Labour Party, but there is little evidence that much change has occurred as yet. The limited support extended by unions to women denies them the crucial access to monetary and other resources enjoyed by men. In 1982, Labour with 11 women M.P.'s had just 25 women on a list of 250 candidates (*Guardian*, April 16, 1982). By 1983, Labour had increased its female representation on candidate lists to 15 percent, resulting in 12.5 percent female candidates, of whom just 10 (of the 78 who ran) were elected (Vallance 1984). As of 1987, of 85, or 16 percent, female candidates nominated, 21 were elected.

In 1982 the Conservative Party had just eight women M.P.'s (of whom one was the prime minister). In the past, according to Hills (1978:12–14), the Conservative Party may have attracted more women candidates than the

---

*All election data for 1987 were made available by Peter McNally, British Information Service, New York.

Labour Party (perhaps more a function of class than party policy), but that did not seem to be the case in 1982. A centralized party office keeps a list of approved candidates. In 1982, of 600 names on the list, only 10 percent were women (down from 15 percent in 1977) (*Guardian*, July 18, 1982). The Conservatives shortlisted 10 percent female candidates, with 6.3 percent (or 40) selected, resulting in an increase to 13 female M.P.'s (Vallance 1984). In 1987 the party nominated 36 women, or 7 percent (a continued decrease), with 17 being elected.

The new Social Democratic Party (SDP) has recruited women discontented with the other parties' attitudes and practices, and its National Steering Committee has adopted two of three women-sponsored resolutions. These resolutions mandate that women be included on every shortlist (at least two of nine candidates) and that four of the eight members on the party's National Steering Committee be women. A mail ballot to party members resulted in the defeat (by 57 percent of the voters) of a resolution requiring equal representation by sex to the party's central decision-making body, the Council for Social Democracy (interview, Toynbee, July 1982). Despite this defeat, the SDP has gone a bit further than its better-established partisan colleagues in meeting some feminist demands for sharing power and issue concerns. Together with the Liberals, the SDP has disseminated endorsements of far-reaching policy changes related to women, including better child-care provisions, strengthening of antidiscrimination legislation, parental leave, and rights for part-time workers (Coote and Campbell 1987: 149). The SDP and its Alliance partner, the Liberals, also sought to increase female representation in 1982. The SDP nominated 17 percent women to its shortlists, resulting in 14.4 percent female candidates, of whom, however, none won (Vallance 1984)! In 1986 the Alliance nominated 100 women (SDP, 20 percent; Liberals, 13 percent), although only two were elected. The Alliance and the Labour Party, apparently competing for the women's vote, thus nominated increasing numbers of women. The SDP threat (supported by pre-election surveys), though not yet translated into electoral power, may have galvanized Labour in particular to adopt a more "feminist" perspective in the most recent election.

Summary of British Women's Role in Parties

Each party seems to be firmly committed to the continuation of separate women's committees. These committees are endorsed by feminists as an important forum through which demands may be articulated and attention focused on women's issues. In each case, feminist party activists would like to see women's groups play a stronger consultative role. Dahlerup and Gulli (1985: 19) have suggested that separate women's organizations within parties have five purposes: 1) to get women to support the party, 2) to recruit women members to the party, 3) to activate women and train them for top party posts, 4) to influence party policy, and 5) to create linkages to women in other groups. Apparently few, if any, of these aims have been achieved by women's organizations in British parties. In Chapter 5, we will examine the degree to which separate Swedish women's organizations within four of the five major parties have affected nominations, party policy, and recruitment to leadership roles.

It seems that only limited benefits have accrued to British women as a result of separatist organization in parties. In 1973 the merits of retaining a separate women's conference were debated at the Labour Party Conference meeting, and its continued existence was endorsed as a mechanism to provide encouragement and training for female activists, as well as to promote solidarity (Holland 1984:62–63). However, women remain underrepresented in policy-making and leadership roles at all levels. In any event, parties appear to provide less of a link to policy-making in a system, such as the British one, increasingly controlled by bureaucratic functionaries. In addition, the hierarchical, mass-based structure of party groups in the United Kingdom is antithetical to the ideals of women's liberation, and so the relationship between many women and party activism is at best ambivalent.

While women in parties have called for mandated positive action with regard to candidate selection—as most obstacles to women's selection appear to exist at the local level—little change has occurred. In response to pressure, the parties have moved toward expressions of greater concern for the nomination of women, but they have not insisted on equality of representation in the final selection process or in any other aspect of party politics. The ability of the 300 Group to attract over 1,500 women to training sessions for political activism points to the continuing gap between rhetoric and reality in much of British party politics. As an all-party group that defies traditional British political dictates, its endurance and continuing appeal say a great deal.

Parties: United States

Political parties are less central to the political process in the United States than in Britain, and feminist interest groups such as the NWPC, NOW, and other groups

have played an important role in recruiting women
for political office, providing training and some campaign support, and actively campaigning for key political issues such as abortion rights and the ERA. In the
United States, the tradition of separate women's groups
and the principle of numerical reservation of seats for
women in the party hierarchy within the parties have
largely been viewed as anachronistic. However, in the
Democratic Party, women moved to mandate equal representation of male and female convention delegates via
the 1972 McGovern-Fraser guidelines. The 1972 Democratic Convention had 40 percent female delegates, while
the Republican Convention had 30 percent (up from 17
percent in 1968). Since then, women's task forces in
both parties have pressed for women's concerns within
the parties and the provision of some funding and training for women candidates (Mandel 1982:211–13). After
the numbers of women delegates to conventions fell
somewhat in 1976, the Democratic Party in 1978–80
moved to equalize convention representation by men
and women and to provide support for such key feminist concerns as the ERA, election of more women to
state and local offices, and even abortion rights. At the
same time, the Reaganite Republican Party moved further to the right and away from commitment to feminist concerns. Nonetheless, in 1984, 48 percent of Republican delegates were women, as were about half of
the Democratic delegates (Freeman 1987:236), an apparent response in both parties to Democratic-inspired
rules reforms.

The increasing significance of feminist interest groups
in the Democratic Party has been particularly striking
during the past decade. Jo Freeman has pointed to the
different political cultures that dominate the Republi-

can and Democratic parties. In the Republican Party, power flows from the top down and delegates' relationship to party leaders and loyalty to the party itself tend to be significant. In contrast, in the Democratic Party, constituencies are seen as the party's building blocks, and power flows from the bottom up (ibid., 232). These cultural distinctions help explain the important role feminist groups have been able to gain in the Democratic Party. In the Republican Party a Woman's Division was created in 1983, joining the (virtually defunct) National Federation of Republican Women, but its major functions were to mobilize, recruit, and publicize party accomplishments rather than to work as an advocacy group within the party. In fact, in the Republican Party, feminists are viewed as having competing loyalties and have been eliminated from leadership and administrative roles (ibid., 235–42). Instead, right-winger Phyllis Schlafly has become the major policy arbiter on women's issues.

In the Democratic Party, because of the different structure and mechanism for representation, feminist groups came to have a major role. Building initially on the turmoil surrounding the 1968 convention, which opened the Democratic Party to reform, feminists gained one vice chair for their ranks (one each also went to blacks and Hispanics) (ibid.). In 1976, disturbed by the falloff in female representation, feminist groups, especially the NWPC, together with the Women's Caucus of the Democratic National Committee and NOW, fought for a 50–50 rule guaranteeing equal representation to women and men. The Carter campaign, initially hostile to this idea, eventually acquiesced. Apparently Carter operatives felt that their refusal to support these feminist concerns would lead to a pro-Kennedy move. By 1980, over 20 percent of the Democratic delegates were members of NOW or of the NWPC (ibid., 230). They gained support for a proposal to deny Democratic Party funds to any candidate who did not support the ERA. NARAL, like the NWPC, had its own floor operation and lobbied successfully for the addition of another minority plank to the platform—one supporting government funding for abortions for poor women (ibid.).

Therefore, by 1984, feminists had demonstrated their political clout. NOW met with five of the Democratic presidential candidates and pressed them on their support for women's issues, female appointments, and willingness to select a female vice presidential candidate. NOW Vice President Mary Jane Collins was appointed to the platform-drafting committee and given the leading role on matters of concern to NOW (Freeman 1985). A coalition of women's groups presented a list of acceptable female vice presidential candidates to Walter Mondale (who had earlier received the endorsement of NOW and later got that of NWPC and NARAL as well). After the nomination of Geraldine Ferraro, a committed feminist, the feminist coalition had little to do at the convention itself.

At the time of this writing, it is not clear how Republican (and some Democratic) efforts to label feminism as an electoral liability—because of its identification as a "special interest" and because of the failure to deliver a "gender gap" vote on behalf of Ferraro—will affect feminist access to power at future Democratic Party conventions (Freeman 1987 : 242).

Despite real gains in representation and support for women's issues (at least in the contemporary Democratic Party), the role of convention politics in the American policy-making process is limited and marginal at best. In addition, numerous (if not most) women seeking political office at all levels in the United States have by-passed traditional centers of candidate support and sought other routes to elective and appointive office. This contention is confirmed by a recent study of female candidates appointed to political office in state government: party-related factors were important for less than a third, with only 15 percent indicating that efforts by state and national party leaders had been very important (Carroll 1984:102). Younger women perceived party leaders as having played virtually no role in their appointments and, in contrast to some of their older female colleagues, had almost no history of party activism or campaign activity (ibid., 103). Crucial to women candidates is a network of women's political organizations, which provide financial aid, research and information, and financial campaign assistance, and generally encourage women's active participation in the political process. Especially prominent in this regard are the Women's Campaign Fund (WCF) and NWPC (Bomafede 1986:2178).

In the United States, once a candidate is elected to political office, partisanship is only one influence that defines his or her political behavior. In Britain, only the 300 Group, an all-party organization that trains and recruits women who wish to run for political office, is analogous to the American model (especially the NWPC).

In the United Kingdom it can no longer be claimed that the women's vote is more "conservative" than men's nor that women are more conservative in their political attitudes, but neither can it be claimed that they are more left-wing. To the degree that a "gender gap" is emerging in Britain it does not represent the result of a feminist organizing effort. What it does seem to represent is a slight movement away from the two major parties, neither of which has met feminist aspirations effectively (Norris [1988]:13; Edgell and Duke 1983: 357–76; Rogers 1983:159).

In the United States, what had appeared to be a significant "gender gap" in 1980, involving female rejection of Reaganite social policy and, in particular, opposition to defense spending and support for domestic spending, was reduced in 1984 to 8 percent in the presidential race, although still providing evidence that fewer women supported Reagan (Light and Lake 1985: 105). Nonetheless, despite the feminist movement's role in gaining a place for Ferraro on the ticket and efforts to mobilize against Reaganite conservatism, at the national level this strategy was not effective in attracting a majority of women voters. Feminist efforts in congressional elections and the women's vote at state and local levels in 1984 and 1986 resulted in greater evidence for the existence of a gender gap.

Unions: Britain

An early link between trade unions and the "new feminism" was evident in Britain in the 1970s. The NCCL held a conference in 1974 that brought together some 550 representatives of women's groups and labor, which was followed by the London Trade's Council's issuance of a ten-point Working Women's Charter drawn up by Communist Party feminists (Coote and Campbell 1987: 56). Nonetheless, what appeared to be a promising relationship has not developed into a set of positive, concrete developments for feminist activists. In contrast to the United States, where about 15 percent of women are union members (fewer than 20 percent of all workers are unionized) and women compose about 30 percent of union membership, in Britain about 31 percent of women are union members and they account for about 40 percent of union membership (fewer than 50 percent of all workers are unionized) (Milkman 1985:300; Ellis 1981; Equal Opportunities Commission 1983a:11). Swedish women, reflecting the national trends, are among the most highly unionized in the world, despite their extensive part-time status.

In Britain, as well as the United States, the number of women unionizing has increased dramatically in the last decade. Of 12 million British TUC members in 1980, about 4 million were women (TUC 1982). Female union membership increased from 1961 to 1980 by 111 percent, while male membership increased by only 17.6 percent (Coote and Campbell 1987).

While many socialist and nonaligned feminists have organized autonomously in their local communities and sought to develop specific feminist projects and activities—shelters for battered women, day-care facilities, self-help clinics, and the like—other socialist feminists have sought to forge links with trade unions in order to reach out to working-class women. Nonetheless, because of the largely middle-class composition of the movement, the separatist ideas that some union women find abhorrent, and the lack of time that plagues many working-class women, it has often been difficult for the women's movement to make headway with its working-class sisters (Hart 1982:161). It is unusual in Britain for campaigning organizations such as feminist groups to have links to trade union politics; particularly at the local level, there is suspicion of women's liberation (ibid.). But there has been an increase in exchange of ideas between union and other feminist women,

Table 3.

Representation of Women in Unions and the Labour Party

Union*	Female Members (% of total)	NEC (Women and Total)	Full-Time Officers (Women and Total)	TUC (Women and Total)	Labour Party Delegates (Women and Total)
TGWU	15.5	0/39	7/500	4/82	1/40
GMWU	34	0/40	13/243	4/74	4/63
AEUW	13.5	7 nonvoting seats/66	1 district secretary	1/37	NA
USDAW	62	3/16	None	5/38	5/34
NUTGW	90	5/15	8/43	12/17	NA
NUPE	66	8/26	6/125	9/32	6/18
NALGO	50	14/69	11/165	11/72	NA**
NUT	72	4/44	17/110	4/34	NA
CPSA	73	12/28	4/NA	10/36	NA
ASTMS	17.5	2/24	6/63	4/31	5/28
TASS	15	NA	NA	4/18	2/17
APEX	56	1/15	1 national, 1 area/of 51	4/15	1/6

SOURCE: *Women's Fightback*, March 1982: 6–7.

*TGWU   Transport and General Workers Union
GMWU   General and Municipal Workers Union
AEUW   Amalgamated Union of Engineering Workers
USDAW   Union of Shop, Distributive, and Allied Workers
NUTGW   National Union of Tailors and Garment Workers
NUPE   National Union of Public Employees

NALGO   National and Local Government Officers' Association
NUT   National Union of Teachers
CPSA   Civil and Public Services Association
ASTMS   Association of Scientific, Technical, and Managerial Staff
TASS   Technical and Supervisory Section [of engineers' union]
APEX   Association of Professional, Executive, Clerical, and Computer Staff

** Not available.

facilitated by such groups as NAC and the NCCL, which have ties to both.

Efforts to politicize newly organized women workers (especially in white-collar unions, where their numbers have greatly expanded) have met with some success, and socialist feminists have gained support for some key issues from the trade unions. But, in the main, women have virtually no power in unions and have been unable to alter existing patterns of low pay and job segregation. Women lack representation in key union committees, among full-time officers, and at the local shop level as stewards and district committee members.

A 1980 survey by Coote and Kellner (1981) showed that while 38 percent of union members surveyed were women, only 11 percent of the executive members, fewer than 6 percent of the full-time officials, and under 15 percent of delegates to the TUC in these unions were women. Of 1,600 trade union officials, only 90 were women in 1983 (Holland 1984:66).

At the 1981 TUC annual meeting, 116 of 1,188 delegates were women, and at the 1983 meeting, 121 of 1,155 (Trades Union Conference 1982:1; *New Statesman*, March 23, 1984). Although a number of unions have a majority of women workers, men remain in control of top positions in individual unions and the TUC. For example, the National Union of Education, with 70 percent female membership, had only four women members on the Executive Committee of 44 in 1980. Several major unions, including the two largest, the Transport and General Workers Union (TGWU) and the General and Municipal Workers Union (GMWU) have not a single female executive member among them (Coote and Campbell 1987:52, 67, 145–67). (See Table 3.)

Feminists have sought greater influence in two ways.

One approach, as in parties, has been to advocate "positive action/positive discrimination," retaining or establishing set-aside or statutory seats on executive committees and seeking other types of special representation, through advisory committees, women's conferences, and the like. In some instances, such efforts do not represent a "new approach"; in the TUC, the Women's Advisory Committee and annual women's conference date back to the 1920s and 1930s, respectively (Randall 1982). In 1920 the Women's Trade Union League (WTUL), a women's labor union, merged with the TUC in return for two protected seats on the TUC Executive Committee. At the same time, another militant women's union, the National Federation of Women Workers, merged with what is now the TGWU. (In short order, the number of women officials fell from 16 to one. It has been an uphill struggle to regain strength ever since [Rogers 1983:31; Lorwin and Boston 1984:145].) In the late 1920s the TUC Women's Conference was created, essentially establishing a group without power. As is true for parties, advisory committees have a solely consultative role and depend on the (often lacking) sympathy of general councils and other policy-making bodies for acceptance. The TUC Women's Action Committee has ten members appointed by the General Council and eight appointed by the Women's Conference; hence, like similar party-related bodies, it is not truly representative of women activists (Breitenbach 1981). In 1981 the TUC, to which most British unions are affiliated, responded to a Women's Conference demand by increasing the number of statutory delegate places reserved for women on the TUC Executive Committee from two to five (out of 41).

However, among the white-collar unions, whose female membership is growing especially rapidly, there have been efforts to create special opportunities for women. Some unions have appointed a national women's officer (e.g., the Technical and Supervisory Section [TASS], of the engineers' union). Others have introduced the practice of setting aside executive council seats for women. Still others, including the GMWU and the Association of Scientific, Technical, and Managerial Staff (ASTMS), have established women's advisory committees or set up equal opportunities groups or women's rights groups at the district level. Even consciousness-raising and special-training sessions for women have been introduced into several unions—including the GMWU, TASS, and the TUC. But, in the main, what has distinguished these efforts has been their "from the top down" quality. In Britain, unlike the situation in Italy and, to a degree, in France, consciousness-raising and feminist groups did not emerge in the workplace (Elliott 1983:68–69). Except in a few instances (as in NALGO and the ASTMS, where several local women's groups were established, and in unions providing women-run courses "for women only"), most women's committees and efforts are institutionalized, segregating their concerns and removing them from grass-roots feminism (ibid.). The lack of a tradition of autonomous women's labor organizations, like those in other European countries and in the United States (to be discussed shortly), has lessened the impact of these efforts. The tensions created by efforts to develop autonomy yet gain influence have not seriously been addressed by trade union feminists in Britain.

The second approach feminists in unions have taken to increase their influence is their drive to gain union support for feminist-related issues. Even in the 1960s, prior to the activization of feminism, the TUC had lobbied for the Equal Pay Act. Later, prompted in part by the 1974 Working Women's Charter—the London-based effort to promote a minimum set of feminist demands in trade unions—the TUC set about revamping its own charter, "Aims for Women at Work." The feminist campaign for child care found expression in the TUC's Charter for Under Fives (1978), calling for comprehensive and universal child care and flextime. The TUC has recognized the "outdated" concept of the family wage and has called for positive action in employment and education. A 1979 TUC ten-point "Charter for Equality" for trade union women advocated special efforts to include women on decision-making bodies and supported child care and awareness-training programs to aid in increasing women's union participation. In addition, the TUC has held conferences on women's issues, established guidelines for positive action in employment, and taken an active role in supporting amendments to the Equal Pay and Sex Discrimination acts.

A dramatic instance of union support for feminist issues came in a massive demonstration—a joint TUC-feminist march in 1979—to protest the possibility of restrictive antiabortion legislation, then pending in the House of Commons in the Corrie Bill. This demonstration marked a unique expression of union support that moved beyond the rhetorical level to practical action.

In 1983, partially owing to pressure from the Labour Party Women's Action Committee, the biennial conference of the largest union in the country, the TGWU, supported a series of resolutions on positive action, including "a call for the extension and formal constitution of effective womens' organizations" in the union and in the Labour Party. It also instructed the union's Labour delegation to support proposals designed to improve women's access to and participation in the party (*Spare Rib*, Sept. 1983:29). This action represented a victory because trade union feminists mobilized the delegates in opposition to the proposed platform, voted down a compromise proposal, and successfully pushed for a strong program of positive action (Rogers 1983:31).

Nonetheless, with regard to key feminist demands (also endorsed by the TUC and other unions)—equal job opportunity for women and an end to pay discrimination—only limited progress has been made. As suggested earlier, male dominance still exists in the unions at all levels, from regional councils to the shop floor to the industry-wide negotiating teams. In crucial negotiations with employers and with the federal government, bargaining priorities related to women have been neglected. The gap between stated policy in resolutions and its implementation in agreements and at the local and plant levels remains a key hurdle for union women (interview, Turner, July 1982). Hence, while unions have provided rhetorical support for "social issues" of concern to working women (e.g., abortion, welfare, housing benefits, day care), their impact has been minimal on economic and industrial matters such as pay and maternity leaves. It is those matters over which men still retain firm control and discretion, limiting possibilities for the implementation of the numerous resolutions passed in union conferences. To a large degree, women's interests are viewed as secondary to the larger concern for social and economic issues. The resulting subordination of feminist demands leaves male bastions of power and sexism untouched (Scott 1982; Bouchier 1984). The indifference with which unions treat women is reflected in a survey that found clear hostility to unions among women factory workers. They articulated the view that unions cared only for men (e.g., holding shop meetings early in the morning) and pointed to the exclusion from unions of part-time workers who are disproportionately female (Speakman 1984:44–45). Policies such as affirmative action ("positive discrimination") have been met with hostility and suspicion owing to high unemployment and concern for male jobs (Lewis 1983: 221).

Several conclusions appear in order. The first is that, in the main, trade unions are unwilling to extend their purported support of feminist concerns to meaningful action in concrete areas. While they have endorsed and supported legislation related to women, they have usually not translated such support to other arenas of power. Although most unions are affiliated to the Labour Party, and effectively control its policies through their majority of votes, they have neither pressed for greater representation for women nor supported other efforts that increase women's power in the party. Nor have their representatives (female or male) on public bodies, such as the EOC (to be discussed in Chapter 4), been advocates on behalf of women's concerns. Hence, there is a need to move beyond the current stage of rhetorical support to a broadened perception of feminist issues in the unions themselves and in the larger society. As Labourite Audrey Wise has said, the aim of feminists is to feminize general issues of policy and generalize issues that are currently defined as women's issues (Perrigo 1985:143). (In Chapter 5, we will see that the situation of Swedish women in trade unions has been similar to that of their British counterparts, with the dominant Swedish union being even more reluctant to deal with feminist demands in a climate that discourages "conflictual" grass-roots activity.) Given the analysis presented here, it is difficult to justify Hewlett's (1986:170) contention that the most effective women's groups in Britain are in parties and unions—not in separate feminist organizations. In addition, though women's committees, equal opportunity officers, and the like exist in most unions, their failure thus far to alter power relations and policy priorities leads to the conclusion, to be explored later, that autonomous women's groups, which organize outside the union structure, may have the best opportunity to produce meaningful change.

Unions: United States

Women compose 16 percent of the unionized labor force in the United States. If employee associations are included (in a work force that is less than 20 percent unionized), the number rises to 30 percent (Milkman 1985:304). As in Britain, the percentage of women currently unionizing is greater than that of men, although total membership in unions is declining precipitously. Like their British counterparts, few American women appear in leadership ranks, one exception being the National Education Association (NEA), a predominantly female union in which they constitute a majority of the board (ibid., 306).

In the International Ladies Garment Workers Union (ILGWU), where they also compose over three-fourths of the membership, they hold 25 percent of the board positions. In public sector unions, such as the American Federation of State, County, and Municipal Employees (AFSCME), which is 40 percent female, women's increasing membership and their participation in union activities have resulted in more of them running for office and becoming shop stewards (Bell 1985:288). In

Table 4.
Female Membership and Leadership in Labor Organiza-
tions with 250,000 or More Women Members, 1978

Organization	Women Members	Percent Female	Women Officers and Board Members	Percent Female
National Education Association	1,219,500	75	5	55
International Brother-hood of Teamsters	480,974	25	0	0
United Food and Com-mercial Workers	480,105	39	2	3
American Federation of State, County and Municipal Employees	408,000	40	1	3
Amalgamated Clothing and Textile Workers' Union	130,660	66	6	15
Service Employees International Union	312,500	50	7	15
International Brother-hood of Electrical Workers	303,518	30	0	0
American Federation of Teachers	300,000	60	8	25
International Ladies Garment Workers Union	278,704	80	2	7
Communication Work-ers of America	259,112	51	0	0

SOURCE: Coalition of Labor Union Women 1980: Tables 3 and 5.

1982, 33 percent of local presidents were women—up from 25 percent seven years before. In 1982, women also held 45 percent of local union offices (ibid.). Within the last few years, a woman was elected international vice president of the Service Employees International Union

(SEIU), which has an estimated 45 percent women members, while two women were elected to the international board of the AFSCME. The SEIU held a conference in 1981 to discuss women's issues such as organizational roles, leadership, and collective bargaining; and several unions, particularly SEIU and AFSCME, have been active in fighting in the courts for women's concerns such as pregnancy disability insurance and comparable worth.

In general, women hold an increasing number of local-level union positions as stewards and officers—though there are still many more female secretaries than presidents. More women have been elected to high office and more resolutions passed on women's recruitment and promotion. Nonetheless, women do not hold top leadership positions in any unions and make up only a small minority of executive board members (Wertheimer 1984:298). In 1978, women held 31 of 655 elective or appointed offices in unions affiliated with the AFL-CIO and 109 of 662 positions in unaffiliated unions and employee associations. They constituted 7.2 percent of national executive board members in AFL-CIO affiliates and 35.3 percent of board members in employee associations where female membership is over twice that in traditional unions (ibid.).

Women's caucuses and committees have been created in a number of unions, and feminist activity has spurred a new interest in union activism among many women workers. Women in the ILGWU and the American Postal Workers Union (APWU) organized to gain support at union conventions for such issues as affirmative action (ibid., 309). Elsewhere, women's divisions have pressed for increased child-care and flextime provisions. As in Britain, the class separation between the larger feminist movement and the working-class women involved in union politics has resulted in considerable distance between these two groups. Nonetheless, despite a reluctance of union women to identify with "women's lib," they have adapted consciousness-raising and other innovative feminist techniques and have been especially interested in issues of gender equality in the labor force (Milkman 1985:307, 309). Efforts to organize around women's issues within unions have most often come from women themselves rather than from union leaders.

However, an aversion to the creation of special interests within unions, as well as the persistence of "male culture," has prevented women from gaining access to substantial internal power in unions, although as in Britain, the trade union movement has become an important ally of the women's movement in the political process. In the United States this support has gone beyond lobbying for legislation to active coalition participation in the Leadership Conference for Civil Rights and similar groups, in which the two movements have in many instances developed a joint agenda for policy. Such coalitional activity has been especially valuable with regard to the legal process and intervention in the administrative sector.

It has become evident that women compose a large segment of unorganized workers and, more importantly, are likelier than males to join unions. Evidence also indicates that unions win more representational elections when they stress women's issues (ibid., 310). Unions have therefore become more receptive to such issues, as they assess their options in a situation of crisis and decline.

However, the American tradition of feminist autonomy from established groups is evident in relationships with the trade union movement as well as with parties.

Feminists have organized within—but also outside—
the labor movement. As in Britain, a tradition of wom-
en's worker groups, such as the WTUL, gave rise to networks of women at the perimeter of the organized trade
union movement (Kessler-Harris 1985:131; Hyman 1985:
24). But while some groups, such as the Coalition of Labor Union Women (CLUW), operate within the traditional labor structure, an alternate approach to organizing, untested in Britain, continues to exist outside the
American unions.

CLUW

In 1974, after a set of legal challenges to force unions to
comply with provisions of antidiscrimination measures
(particularly the Civil Rights Act of 1964), the leading
arm of the American labor movement, the AFL-CIO,
helped establish a women's caucus within its ranks—
CLUW. Like women's groups within British unions,
CLUW has pressed for greater sensitivity to women's
concerns, increased representation in leadership circles,
and an end to job discrimination. (In addition, it lobbies
for legislation and aids in organizing potential women
union members.) CLUW has created a women's base
and forum for networking within the labor movement,
and the result has been more representation of women
in union offices and the creation of women's departments and committees in some unions. CLUW has taken
the union structure as a given, with the goal of advancing women's interests as workers and unionists within it
(Milkman 1985:310). Membership in CLUW is limited
to those who were already both union members and activists in the trade union movement along traditional
lines (e.g., elected leadership and committees). Thus,
CLUW functions as a means to network within union

circles, creating pressure to act on women's demands. In the main, the group has served as a mechanism to promote women into leadership ranks; its chapters rarely include the union rank and file (ibid., 312). At present, CLUW's membership comprises only about 1 percent of union women members, themselves a minority of union workers. As currently constituted, the group serves best as an internal union "watchdog," effective at leadership levels and only nominally attentive to the unorganized and the rank and file (ibid., 315).

Like its British counterparts, the CLUW has largely met with an uneven response. Progress in increasing the representation of women in leadership ranks has been slow, but one visible result of CLUW's efforts was the selection of Joyce Miller in 1980 as the first woman on the AFL-CIO's executive council. Although union support has been generated for such issues as the ERA and the Pregnancy Discrimination Act and for coalitions formed to promote them, there has been limited progress in gaining support for matters like affirmative action. (In Britain the rhetorical level of support for some issues appears to be greater.) With 16,000 members and 72 local chapters, CLUW operates within the constraints of labor union politics and has avoided confrontation with the union hierarchy (Goodin 1983:146).

A Second Route to Organizing Women Workers

In the United States a second tradition of organizing labor women has developed, owing in part to the ambivalence of many professional Americans toward the organized labor movement and perhaps also to the absence of a vigorous socialist (feminist) presence. This alternate route involves independent organizations of working women, primarily white-collar workers—groups like

Wider Opportunities for Women (WOW), Working Women, and Union WAGE. Unlike unions that concentrate on collective bargaining, these groups seek to enforce antidiscrimination and affirmative action legislation, demonstrate against employers, and engage in educational efforts to promote safety, organization, and job rights (Seifer and Wertheimer 1979:168; Gelb and Klein 1983:34). As unions have perceived the growing strength of autonomous groups of women workers, they have sought to establish links with them, such as the relationship recently forged between Working Women (office workers) and the SEIU, which created a new union, District 925, to organize women.

In the 1970s, a younger group of feminist activists, who had roots in the New Left and the seminal women's liberation movement but who were also critical of labor politics, organized among previously uninvolved office workers. The group Working Women, formerly called 9 to 5, was a particularly successful result. Rather than dealing directly with unionization, this group concentrated on consciousness-raising and public dramatization of issues involving union organizations as well as on developing participatory democracy (Milkman 1985: 315). After 1975, Working Women moved closer to the organized union movement when Local 925 was organized in conjunction with the SEIU. The new "union" was charged with organizing office workers all over the country and, although a part of the SEIU structure, drew staff direction from Working Women and retained autonomy within the union structure (ibid.). Working Women has continued as a separate entity outside the union as well. In addition to concentrating on unionization, it has focused on other issues of concern to women, including age discrimination and bank and insurance company relations with women workers. The group's emphasis on participation by all members continues and visible public actions, involving media attention, are utilized (ibid., 316). In its emphasis on developing specifically female organizational forms and concerns, Working Women seems to be almost a direct descendant of the WTUL.

The dilemma for autonomous groups is how to maintain independence while at the same time influencing the larger union structure. If the Working Women experiment proves successful, it may point the way to the creation of a uniquely feminist worker's presence, with influence in the union and access to its resources and power.

Another approach to women's employment is WOW (Wider Opportunities for Women), which grew from a locally focused volunteer organization stressing part-time work to a national nonprofit organization with several staff members. WOW has sought to combine service and advocacy, providing training programs and job placement in nontraditional occupations. Through monitoring, coalition building, and advocacy, as well as publicizing and documenting job inequity, WOW and other groups have sought to reach women who are not union members and are outside the traditional labor market (Fleming 1983). The independent tradition continues and autonomous groups of working women, together with groups such as WOW and Catalyst, have been active in finding jobs for women in all levels of the economic ladder and in fighting job discrimination.

**Local Women's Committees: "Municipal Feminism"—
A New Direction in British Politics?**

Recent efforts at the local level of British politics suggest that in some instances it may be possible for feminist women to work closely with Labour councils and local authorities. New developments in numerous British urban areas have interacted effectively with the decentralized structure of British feminism. Since 1969, a variety of multifaced action groups have developed in many British urban centers, focusing on feminist collectives, rape crisis centers and shelters for battered women, health clinics, black women's groups, and groups of women in law, the media, and other professions (Bouchier 1984). Feminists have turned to local council governments for funding, access, and space to maintain their activities; and, fearing hierarchy and male co-optation, they have tended to prefer local-level dialogues to those at the national level. Since 1982, aided in part by the increased number of local councilors who are women (18.4 percent) (Equal Opportunities Commission 1983a:95), several local councils have created women's committees to promote representation of women and women's interests (Goss 1984). Such committees have been established by the Greater London Council (GLC), numerous London boroughs, including Camden, Islington, Southwark, and Hackney, and by 22 other British urban centers (including some in Scotland). Virtually all these constituencies are under Labour Party domination. In some communities, support for women's committees came from local councilors (e.g., London), while in others the initiative for commission establishment emanated from the women's movement itself. In Leeds, for example, a local conference that drew together Labour Party and SDP women, trade union members, and local women's groups (including Rape Crisis, Asian Women, and the 300 Group) resulted in the formation of a women's Subcommittee of the Policy and Resources Committee (Flannery and Roelofs 1984). This body strengthened the work already begun by the Women's Equal Employment Group, which had been established in 1982 by trade union and other local women. By 1984, the Leeds council had trebled child-care funding (Rowbotham 1984).

The greatest resources were those of the GLC, which in 1984 devoted nearly £8 million to funding local women's groups and projects (interview, Wise, July 1984). The GLC Women's Committee sought to involve a wide spectrum of women by holding open meetings and co-opting women to represent such groups as lesbians, the disabled, and trade unionists (Goss 1984). Funding was given to Greenham Common women for day care and to a female transportation service, as well as to day care and health facilities—all to a generally hostile press reception (Flannery and Roelofs 1984). A major thrust of the GLC Women's Committee was to foster multiaction centers for women, thus bringing some order to the centrifugal politics we have described, perhaps building on the women's action centers that already existed in many British cities (interview, Wise, July 1984). At the GLC, efforts were made to emphasize participatory democracy and openness through public meetings, which received enthusiastic response and enjoyed large attendance (Flannery and Roelofs 1984:77). Meetings were open to all interested women and tasks were rotated, in accordance with feminist theory. Despite media emphasis on funding of "radical" projects, child-care subsidies, in fact, accounted for the bulk of GLC funding efforts.

The GLC budget for grants to women increased from £300,000 in 1982 to over £7 million in 1984 (Goss 1984: 112). Between April and December 1983 alone, 227 projects were funded for a total of £4.5 million, an unusually large infusion of funds for previously impoverished feminist groups (*Spare Rib*, Feb. 1985:20). Nonetheless, the portion allocated to women still was only a fraction of the total GLC 1983–84 budget of £824 million—less than 1 percent, in fact (Livingston 1984:261). However, by 1986, the fourth and final year of the GLC Women's Committee's budget existence, its budget had grown to £90 million (Coote and Campbell 1987:105–8). In this committee, as in other women's committees, local councilors retained the right to outvote and override the interest of the feminist consultants (*Spare Rib*, Feb. 1985: 19–20)—a situation that has led some observers to suggest that in this instance women's groups are relatively autonomous but lack effective power (Goss 1984:125). However, the GLC did provide a meeting place at County Hall for a wide variety of women's activities and purchased a building for the specific use of two feminist groups, A Women's Place and the Women's Research and Resources Center (Rogers 1983:173). In addition, the GLC Women's Committee played a campaigning or mobilizing role, aiding efforts related to working women, child care, and Greenham Common (Flannery and Roelofs 1984:80).

Women's committees established in the London boroughs of Camden and Islington have had varying degrees of success and funding. The Camden group, with strong support from local Labour councilors, has devoted considerable funding to women's efforts. A Woman's Bus has traveled the community to focus discussions and provide information and advice, circumventing the media by going directly to local women (Goss 1984; Flannery and Roelofs 1984). However, in Islington, as of 1984, the Women's Unit was all but defunded and defunct (interview, Potter, July 1984).

The women's committees have been unique in creating new structures that bring women into the political process. They have aimed at breaking down traditional hierarchical processes and, through innovative systems of publicity and participation, tried to seek out women who are not normally part of the political process. They have also attempted to broaden the framework of service provision from a feminist perspective. Some feminists, especially those wary of Labour Party practices in the past, fear that such efforts may co-opt the movement (Goss 1984:128). In fact, however, these committees may act as a bridge between the movement and both labor and governmental structures, if they are successful.

A major drawback to these promising efforts has been the attack of the Conservative government on both the GLC and local London council governments (12 of which have had women's committees) (*Spare Rib*, Feb. 1985: 20). The GLC itself was dissolved in 1986 by the Thatcher government. Although the trend toward local-level support for women's efforts in Britain is still too new to measure, these efforts are notable in providing linkages between traditional, socialist, and radical feminist groups and in seeking to reach out to the vast number of British women who have heretofore been unaffected by the feminist movement. Can local-level priorities be reorganized and feminists given real power rather than just their customary advisory role? Can a *modus vivendi* be reached between feminist democracy and traditional hierarchical government structures? These questions are as yet unresolved.

This chapter has assessed two different approaches to feminist political organizing: the British one, in which movement activity has been contained within the existing parties and unions, and the American one, in which gender-based groups have sought to interact with a weaker party and union system. It seems evident that the British model of organizing women's groups within parties and unions has had only limited impact on representation and policy. Whether, as Coote and Campbell (1987:148) have recently argued, the new forces of radical activism in the Labour Party are sufficient to "break down some of the barriers that had stood between the women's movement and parliamentary politics in the 1970's" is not clear from the analysis presented here.

In the United States, independent groups such as NOW, the NWPC, and NARAL have gained a significant voice in the Democratic Party, pressing their views effectively on a still predominantly male leadership. The role of feminist movements as constituents in electoral politics appears to be clearer from the American case, although in Britain there have been some (more half-hearted?) efforts to mobilize them in order to create new alignments of political power.

Unions in both countries present an ambiguous picture, although in the United States the innovative model created by 9 to 5, emanating from an independent feminist base, has suggested new alternatives for workers and organizers. In Britain a new model of feminist activism, at the local level, has seemed to represent a fresh, more "political phase" of the movement where it has felt most at home. The effect of the abolition of the GLC, which had the most resources and influence of all local committees and working parties, is still undetermined.

In Chapter 5, we will explore the rather different Swedish model of integration into existing structures. But first, we examine the role of feminists in policy-making in Britain and the United States.

4

Feminism in Government: Advocacy and Policy-making

We can test the impact feminists have made on national politics by analyzing public policy issues. We must explore 1) agenda setting—the role of feminist groups in initiating and structuring public policy, 2) the influence of these groups on legislative and executive decision-making, and 3) the implementation of the policies enacted. Central to this analysis is an examination of the role played by feminist groups in any or all of these crucial steps in the policy-making process. Implicit in our discussion will be the question: Have the policies enacted made a difference?

In this chapter we analyze the role of two apparently similar bodies: the Equal Opportunities Commission (EOC) in Britain and the Equal Employment Opportunity Commission (EEOC) in the United States. In addition, we examine the structure of the policy-making process in both countries by focusing on abortion and sex discrimination politics. Finally, we assess the role of British and American feminist groups in affecting policy outcomes by looking closely at the politics of domestic violence, an issue first brought to public consciousness in Britain. In Chapter 5, we will extend the analysis to Sweden.

Not surprisingly, given the institutional setting described in Chapter 1, women are poorly represented in British political life. In 1982, only 23 women served in Parliament, although a record 210 stood for election (European Union of Women 1982). By 1987 a higher number—40 out of 221 candidates—had gained seats.* In addition to the female (though hardly feminist) prime minister, Margaret Thatcher, there are three other women ministers in the present Conservative government, but they do not hold cabinet rank. Of 97 senior judges, only two are women. While women increasingly qualified as barristers and solicitors during the 1970s and 1980s, in England and Wales they composed only 3 percent of the Queens Counsels, from whom judges in the High Court and above are chosen (Lovenduski 1986 : 217). In 1983 only 4 percent of High Court judges were women. No women were represented among the higher-level appeals judges. In the senior civil service, in 1986, fewer than 4 percent of high administrative officers were women. In 1983, while women composed 47.1 percent of Home civil servants, there were no female permanent secretaries (ibid., 216). Few women are nominated to, or serve on, government committees, councils, or other public bodies. And, at the local level, in the mid-1970s there were only two chief women's officers out of 500 (Hills 1981 : 27). But more women are becoming local councilors—in 1982 they numbered 18.4 per-

* Data for 1987 were made available by Peter McNally, British Information Service, New York.

cent (Equal Opportunities Commission 1983a : 95). However, as we noted earlier, the overwhelming structure of power in Britain is predominantly male.

Government-based Advocacy
of Women's Issues in Britain

The Economic Opportunities Commission

During the 1960s and early '70s, pressure arose in Parliament for the creation of a quasi-independent body to "act as an amalgam of recipient and investigator complaints relating to sex discrimination, conciliator where possible and prosecutor in the courts where this failed" (Byrne and Lovenduski 1978 : 157). The result was the creation of the Equal Opportunities Commission to enforce the Equal Pay Act and Sex Discrimination Act (to be discussed shortly). The EOC was given law enforcement powers, research and investigative capacity, and jurisdiction over a number of policy areas related to women (education, housing, and employment) (Meehan 1983b : 70–71). Excluded from EOC jurisdiction were the social security, pensions, taxes, and nationality. It was hoped that the EOC would be a vigorous voice on behalf of women and would play a strong enforcement role. In practice, the EOC has not developed as robust a defender of equal rights as many hoped, although it does provide a forum and base for feminist-related issues, one of the few that exists in a system essentially closed to change-oriented groups.

The EOC is a quango, or quasi-judicial/legislative entity, and as such is not strictly accountable to the House of Commons or the executive branch. The agency therefore apparently has a degree of independence. In the United States, by contrast, appointments to commissions and agencies dealing specifically with women's issues—the Equal Employment Opportunities Commission (EEOC), Commission on Civil Rights, and Office of Civil Rights (formerly at the Department of Health, Education, and Welfare, later at the Department of Education)—are politicized, and feminist groups are consulted and vocal about their preferences.

As a quango, in fact the EOC relies on funding from the Home Office and is dependent on government departments. It also lacks the supportive constituency necessary for a successful confrontationist stance (Atkins and Hoggett 1984:196–97). It is therefore reliant on informal government contacts and, as a result, lacks a public image and awareness. Perhaps mindful of the restrictive role to which the Commission for Racial Equality was limited when it sought to build a stronger relationship with ethnic groups and develop a constituency, the EOC has been more cautious (ibid., 197).

In addition, a history of tripartism limits the role of women both at the EOC and within the judicial process. Secrecy pervades the appointments process and access is limited, except for established groups. Nominations to the agency are made by reference to lists of "The Great and the Good," on which few, if any, women are found; interests represented include those of party, region, and, especially, business and labor. Recommendations of women clearly identified with feminism were rejected until the late 1970s (Meehan 1983b:70–74). Until recently, when two women with a feminist orientation (Sandra Brown and Ann Robinson) were appointed, the commission reflected little input from women per se. In the main, female trade union representatives on the EOC have been more responsive to labor than to women's concerns (interview, Turner, July 1982). Meehan

(1983a:182) points out that when in one instance a TUC representative on the EOC dissented from the union position on protective legislation, she was met with punitive action by the TUC, including denial of reappointment to the EOC and removal from her senior position in the TUC. Leadership roles on the commission have been given primarily to majority party representatives.

In addition to the lack of access to appointments and the policy-making process, the role of the EOC is limited by the neocorporatist structure of the legal system. British employment suits are first heard in industrial tribunals rather than in courts. Tribunals are comprised of representatives of industry and labor and are seen as part of the collective bargaining process (Meehan 1983a). In this process, there is limited representation for complainants by unions or groups similar to the American Civil Liberties Union (ACLU), which do not really exist in the United Kingdom. While the EOC and National Council for Civil Liberties (NCCL) provide some legal aid, there are no *pro bono*, public interest, law-related groups that play an advocacy role on behalf of the disadvantaged. Trade unions, which could aid complainants in bringing suits, usually do not. In addition, tribunal personnel are overworked and undertrained and lack an understanding of sex discrimination issues. The number of cases heard and upheld by tribunals is discouraging to feminist aspirations (a situation we will discuss later). Tribunals do not create case law; therefore their rulings result in a plethora of ad hoc decisions. The British judiciary is naturally conservative, and not surprisingly, has shown itself to be far from progressive on issues of sex discrimination (Jackson 1984: 193) Of the cases that have been won, at least two important ones have been on appeal to the European Court.

Among them was a case of indirect discrimination brought by Belinda Price. She alleged that the Civil Service Commission's requirement of an upper-age limit of 28 for executive officers discriminated against women as childbearers and rearers during their twenties (Bruegel 1983:151).

Because of the limited legal advocacy structure and the tradition of bureaucratic neutrality, outside pressure and monitoring of compliance with the law are absent in the United Kingdom (Meehan 1983a, 1983b). In contrast to the United States, where the existence of policy networks is a key part of the process of influence, in Britain women have not developed similar networks for reasons of ideology and institutional structure. Hence, there has been little or no organization per se to bolster the enforcement of sex discrimination laws.

The style of the 15-person EOC itself has been to limit emphasis on enforcement and sanctions and to concentrate on research and publicity. It has sought to avoid confrontation in favor of consultation and persuasion and has been involved in few, if any, dramatic cases (Meehan 1983b). It has conducted several protracted informal investigations into equal pay and employment issues—with limited outcomes. The House of Lords has prevented the EOC from mounting formal investigations into the general workings of organizations (Atkins and Hodgett 1984:39). As a result, the EOC has sought to influence government at higher levels, by submitting proposals and evidence to the House of Commons and relevant agencies, including royal commissions and agencies concerned with manpower services and education (*Spare Rib*, May 9, 1981). It has provided legal assistance and advice to individuals (its power is limited to *backing* cases brought by individuals) and brought sev-

eral cases to the European Court. Perhaps most significantly, it has played a major role in educating public
opinion on sex discrimination issues (Byrne and Lovenduski 1978a). It has helped create consciousness of the
need for change and has demonstrated the extent of
discrimination. The EOC has issued films as well as
pamphlets and other documents, held conferences, and
played a key role in funding projects, even those of
women's groups considered "radical." Among them
have been grants to the Women's Action Group, the
Women's Health Information Center, the NCCL, Asian
women's groups, Women's Aid, the Women's Therapy
Center, Sisterwrite (a feminist bookshop), the Women's
Research and Resource Center, and unions (for analysis
of sexual harassment) (EOC 1981). In a system where
funding opportunities are limited, the EOC is a new and
important source of financial support for emerging feminist groups.

The EOC may also play a role in building relationships among disparate groups concerned with women's
issues. An example is the commission's large annual
conference, to which 70 to 80 women's organizations are
invited, thus providing a rare forum and meeting place
for a wide variety of feminist activists (interview, Trembath, Aug. 1982).

Additional factors limiting the effectiveness of the
EOC are its location in Manchester (though it does maintain a small London office) and the absence of regional
offices as well as the high turnover rate among its chief
executives—four different heads during its first five
years of existence (interview, Lockwood, Aug. 1982).

The commission has had difficulty in maintaining
traditional bureaucratic neutrality among a staff with
feminist inclinations. The result has been tensions between commissioners and staff—unlike the situation in

its American counterpart, the EEOC, whose staff and groups frequently consult and may be mutually supportive (Meehan 1983a:74). The election of a more sympathetic government would undoubtedly help, considering that the Conservative government cuts forced the EOC to reduce its staff from 400 to 148 (*Guardian*, July 10, 1980). Some British feminists fear that having created a body with extensive purported power, although far less in actual terms, the commission may actually impede further action regarding sex equality (Byrne and Lovenduski 1978a:146). The creation of a feminist alliance that transcends ideological, party, and class bias and that could provide legitimacy for feminist-related concerns may be the only way to strengthen the EOC (Meehan 1983a:74). The EOC itself has concluded that little further progress can be made without "substantial amendment" (Glucklich 1984:108).

The Women's National Commission

A second government-based potential advocacy group in Britain is even more limited by constraints than the EOC. The Women's National Commission (WNC) is a government-founded and sponsored organization that was established in 1969. It has two co-chairs, one government appointed and one elected by the commission itself. The WNC's mission is "to ensure by all possible means that the informed opinion of women is given due weight in government" (WNC 1982). The commission has a requisite size of 50 organizations, which must be national bodies with a large and active membership. Current members include women's sections of unions and parties.

The WNC develops working groups to examine issues and has produced papers, often in response to government (consultative) Green and White papers. While superficially resembling such American federal agencies as the Women's Bureau in the Department of Labor and the commissions on the status of women, the WNC shares some of their weaknesses and then some! The WNC is constrained in its criticism of government because of its close ties to the incumbent administration. In addition, the scope of its membership is limited by the requirement that member groups must have been in existence a number of years and must have a national presence and membership. These ground rules militate against inclusion of most—if not all—women's liberation groups that have no say; hence, the WNC lacks true representativeness of women's interests (interview, Tuomin, July 1982). Even such small London-based groups as the Fawcett Society are excluded by this policy, although nonmember groups are occasionally invited to participate in the WNC's deliberations on an ad hoc basis. In addition, the group's charter lacks a provision for changing its organizational membership. The WNC is run by the general secretary (a civil servant) and one staff member, limiting its role greatly. Moreover, the group's power, like many others discussed here, is strictly advisory. The group exists on a budget that makes up 3 percent of the EOC's (limited) resources (Stott 1978:277). Hence, while the WNC remains as a symbol of women's influence and a potential advocate for women's concerns, which no government will abolish for symbolic reasons, it represents a classic case of institutional powerlessness.

Government-based Advocacy of Women in the United States

In the United States by 1980 the number of women state legislators tripled in 12 years to over 14 percent, although they constituted only 5.1 percent (25 of the 532 members) of Congress (Bomafede 1986:2176). In the 1980s women mayors governed several of America's largest cities, including Houston, Chicago, and San Francisco, and the number of municipal officials who were women tripled (from 1971) to 13 percent (Flammang 1984:10). Especially under the Carter administration, women's fortunes in the administrative sector improved dramatically. The number of women in top policy-making jobs subject to presidential appointment (grades 13–18) increased from a pre-Carter 14 percent to 33 percent in 1979. In cabinet and subcabinet positions, women's representation improved from 4 to 8 percent. Carter also appointed an unprecedented number of women (15.8 percent) as federal judges, bringing female representation on the federal bench to 6.6 percent. Under Ronald Reagan's administration after 1980, however, these numbers dropped significantly to 4.4 percent of judicial nominations and 9 percent of senior federal appointments (Harrison 1984:149; *New York Times*, March 27, 1987:A12). By 1987, Reagan appointments of women to top positions had reached 15 percent, although, despite their gender, many could be classified as antifeminists.

In the United States, as in the United Kingdom, the activities of agencies addressing sex discrimination, especially the EEOC, have been limited by an insufficient budget and bureaucratic ineptitude (Greenburger 1980: 11). Enforcement has been primarily left to individuals who face serious obstacles (lack of money, information, and support) in pursuing sex discrimination cases.

In the United States the Women's Bureau was for some 40 years the focal point for women in government. Its role was hampered to some degree by its advocacy of protective legislation for women and its accompanying antipathy to the ERA (Tinker 1983:11). Nonetheless, after it abandoned its endorsement of protection and came to support the ERA, it became both a resource (as it had been since its inception, providing statistics and data) and an advocacy agency on behalf of women's concerns. It has helped provide resources and a forum for a variety of women's (primarily economic) concerns. However, though at one time it was the only federal agency charged with looking after women's welfare, it has been joined (at various times) by the federal commissions on the status of women, the Civil Rights Commission, and the EEOC. The significance of these bodies has varied with the particular administrative viewpoints and with the type of leadership provided at a given time.

The EEOC was created pursuant to the passage of Title VII of the Civil Rights Act of 1964. As Vicki Randall has pointed out, it initially had fewer formal enforcement powers than its British counterpart, the EOC. Nonetheless, it emerged as a relatively important tool through which major policy advances in equal employment might be made, although its effectiveness has varied with the commitment of different administrations to it. The initial EEOC had power only to seek voluntary compliance with the Civil Rights Act; it could not litigate, although it could file *amicus curiae* briefs. After 1972, largely owing to pressure from the organized feminist movement and from commissioners sympathetic to the movement (whose appointments had been pressed for by the organized women's community), its enforcement powers were strengthened (Randall 1982: 189; Meehan 1983a:177).

For the EEOC, enforcement involves the resolution of individual charges and the elimination of "patterns and practices" of discrimination (ibid.). Executive Order

11375 amends the earlier Executive Order 11246 to include sex discriminatory employment practices among
those prohibited to employers under contract to the federal government. Although the enforcing agency, the Office of Federal Contract Compliance Programs (OFCCP),
has not been vigorous in enforcing policy, a 1969 order
spelled out in detail what affirmative action would en-
tail, in terms of goals, timetables, and monitoring progress. Under pressure from WEAL, the executive orders
were applied to women in higher education as well.

Despite the unevenness of the enforcement process,
nondiscrimination efforts have been aided in the United
States by a variety of factors unavailable to the British
feminist movement. Nonetheless, during most of the
1970s, major questions were raised by critics about the
EEOC's administrative efficiency and the seriousness of
its commitment to end discrimination. The backlog of
unresolved cases seemed particularly indicative of inadequate efforts. But in 1977, Eleanor Holmes Norton, a
new chair appointed by the Carter administration, in-
stituted a complete overhaul of the commission in order
to rationalize its structure and procedures. Even prior
to that, though, the commission had demonstrated its
ability to litigate effectively on behalf of individuals.
Through issuance of guidelines and briefs, it was able in
large measure to shape the nature of judicial response
to the issues raised. Particularly noteworthy was the
1973 settlement with the American Telephone and Telegraph Company (AT&T), the largest such award ever
made under civil rights legislation (ibid., 178). Hundreds of briefs were filed on behalf of individuals and
also in class action suits. In 1977 alone, 35 class action
suits were resolved.

A major factor in the EEOC's ability to change law

was the establishment of a policy network that aided in the appointment of sympathetic staff and commissioners, consulted with the commission, and produced additional legislation to strengthen the functioning of the agency. A Washington women's policy network brought legislators, bureaucrats, staff, and feminist advocates together on a variety of issues. The emergence of the women's movement aided in expanding federal policies, and because the bureaucratic process in the United States is recognized as more explicitly "political" than that of Britain, the effectiveness and persistence of the Washington women's lobby helped to influence appointments, press for continuing antidiscrimination legislation (such as Title IX, banning sex discrimination in education), and monitor agency enforcement (Randall 1982). The appointment of an outspoken black woman leader (Eleanor Holmes Norton) to head the EEOC in 1977 was made in consultation with civil rights and women's groups. "With its *amicus curiae* briefs, strict guidelines and its power to litigate after 1974, the EEOC is thought to have become, in the 1970's, a strong and successful proponent of women's rights" (Meehan 1985:10).

Under the Reagan administration, funding for civil rights enforcement dropped, now constituting only 0.07 percent of the federal budget. The ability of federal agencies to conduct compliance reviews, investigate complaints, and attack discrimination in a systematic fashion has been severely curtailed (Braun 1984:99). Like the British EOC, the EEOC has experienced cutbacks in staff and budget, with clerical staff and legal (attorney) positions most affected. These reductions in turn have slowed the production of documentation needed to prosecute cases. Litigation activities have also been curtailed owing to reduced funding, with little money available for witnesses, special studies, and data processing (ibid.). Staff at the OFCCP has also been cut back, resulting in a backlog of individual complaints (ibid., 100). New regulations further curtail coverage (of small firms) and may discourage the bringing of systemic discrimination suits. For the first time, an administration has intervened as a "friend of the Court" against women and minorities in "reverse discrimination" suits, although the Supreme Court has generally upheld affirmative action in recent cases (*Johnson v. Transit Agency,* Santa Clara County, California). Women have not yet lost most of the equal employment gains of the last two decades, although they have been forced to expend enormous energy and scarce resources just to maintain the status quo. But the resignation under protest of government officials such as Joseph Cooper, responsible for compliance with affirmative action guidelines, have helped highlight the administration's failure to vigorously enforce the law (*New York Times,* Jan. 5, 1987 : II4).

The Contrast Between U.S. and British Advocacy

To the degree that the EEOC has been a more effective force for change than its British counterpart—although its role depends in large measure on the sympathetic support of both the executive and judicial branches— several points of contrast appear significant. First, the federal courts in the United States have upheld and reinforced numerous claims pursued under Title VII. Second, American courts are more available to make and interpret policy and may provide another access route to policy change. Third, class action suits may result in more sweeping and effective remedies, and the growing litigation sector among women's groups has used its limited resources to aid in bringing such suits before the courts.

A final area of contrast is the policy toward affirmative action. Atkins and Hoggett (1984:199) suggest that four factors present in the United States regarding this policy are absent in the United Kingdom: 1) the public availability of requisite statistics, 2) the imposition of high damages in discrimination cases, 3) the powerful position of the EEOC in conciliating and monitoring out-of-court settlements, and 4) the willingness and power of the courts to uphold positive action (or affirmative action) orders. As we shall see, similar constraints limit the effectiveness of Sweden's machinery for equal opportunities. An additional factor limiting the impact of the British EOC may be that its power (and potential constituency) is separated from that of the Commission on Racial Equality (CRE) and its racial and ethnic base, so that joint efforts, such as those facilitated in the United States by the Civil Rights Commission and EEOC, are not feasible in Britain. A possible opening for more effective policy-making by the EOC may lie in its emerging relationship with the EEC, via the European Commission, European Parliament, and European Court of Justice (ibid.; Meehan 1985:189). (In 1984, for example, the EOC finally met its obligations as stated in an EEC directive of 1975, amending the Equal Pay Act to cover equal pay for equal value—or comparable worth, in American terminology.) But despite this potential support for a stronger EOC role, it is difficult to see the emergence of a greatly altered commission unless a more cohesive and politicized feminist movement can effectively intervene at the administrative level (Meehan 1985:189).

The absence of an organized British feminist movement, coupled with an institutional setting that makes monitoring of implementation far more difficult than it is in the United States, helps explain in part the considerably different outcomes in the two nations (Randall 1982:196). In the United Kingdom the ensuing separation between the so-called neutral bureaucracy and feminist activists has both reflected and reinforced the absence of a feminist lobby. In the United States, equal opportunity policies have had a greater impact than in Britain (and Sweden as well, as we shall see in the next chapter) because they have been in effect longer and have been accompanied by more aggressive enforcement of antidiscrimination policies (Dex and Shaw 1986:14).

Women in Power:
Mobilizing Power in the Legislative Arena

Britain

Women as elected political officials may provide support for feminist issues. Consistent with our analysis of the EOC and the EEOC, British women M.P.'s have been reluctant allies of the women's movement, while their American counterparts have developed a bit more cohesion on certain issues of interest to the feminist community. The women in Parliament who became concerned with abortion apparently did so only after a decision was visited on them by their male colleagues (Vallance 1979:88). Once limiting bills were introduced in 1974–75, the M.P.'s were galvanized into action and helped organize support in committees and through petitions, marches, and the like. (In contrast, the Sex Discrimination Act was given qualified support by women M.P.'s

because many of them saw it largely as publicity con-
cocted for International Women's Year [ibid., 93].) But
whatever the momentum created around the abortion
issue, parliamentary women have no very clear and
"certainly no very enduring sense of themselves as a
group" (ibid., 96). The presence of Margaret Thatcher as
the lone woman in her cabinet merely reinforces the
view that there are "exceptional women" who occasionally achieve power and who rule in "splendid isolation"
from their female colleagues. In the House of Commons,
women do not see themselves as having any "esprit de
corps." Most Labour women may have a degree of cama-
raderie and unity of purpose about some, though not all,
issues. The existence of separate Lady Member's Sitting
Rooms by party has developed in recent years, accen-
tuating partisan differences between women M.P.'s. In
the House of Lords as well, party is a greater influence
on behavior than is sex. Women peers are not united by
a feminist ideology, nor have they provided any feminist
input in Parliament (Drewry and Brock 1983:2).

In contrast, in the United States a congressional Caucus for Women's Issues founded in 1977 claimed a bipartisan membership of 127 (down to 96 in 1986—83
Democrats and 13 Republicans [Bomafede 1986:2176]),
including a majority of men (Thompson 1984:2). The
group acts as a lobbying organization, with a bipartisan
leadership and an all-female executive committee. The
caucus aids in gaining electoral support for members
and provides information to its constituents through a
newsletter, *Update.* It prepares news releases and promotes legislation through meetings with administration officials and through media advocacy efforts. The
caucus may be weakened by its somewhat partisan cast,
and its failure to solicit support from all women mem-

bers (of the 24 female members of Congress, two Democrats and seven Republicans are not members).

However, though women legislators in the United States do not necessarily or even usually behave as a bloc, studies have found that women are consistently more liberal, particularly on issues concerning women and consumer protection (Norris [1986]:6). Republican women and men in Congress exhibit contrasting behavior on such issues as abortion rights, child benefits, and the ERA (ibid., 9). Women legislators also appear to favor decreased military expenditures and arms control, regardless of party affiliation. In this context it may prove especially significant that the caucus supports legislation such as that contained in the Economic Equity Act (EEA). The group has served as a source of information and consensus building (as it apparently did in the successful drive for Child Support Enforcement legislation in 1984 [Thompson 1984:22]).

The Policy Process

Britain

Pym (1974:80–81) suggests that few promotional pressure groups have a meaningful impact on the policymaking process in the United Kingdom, although she views the case of abortion reform as having been almost unique. Most legislation relating to women has been submitted as a private member's bill, and depends on tacit to overt government support for passage. The House of Lords and appointed select committees have often played a key role in mobilizing support for "women's" legislation. Many feminists in Britain are skeptical about the ability of equal rights campaigns and legislation to alter the balance of power between men and women (Perrigo 1985:137). Hence the passage of the Equal Pay Act (EPA) and subsequent Sex Discrimination Act (SDA) owed more to the parties, the TUC, and also the EEC (whose Article 119, promulgated in 1957, provided for equal pay for equal work) than it did to the women's movement. Women's groups have played an auxiliary—but not central role—in creating support for legislative enactments.

The EPA was enacted under the aegis of a Labour government committed after 1964 to the principle of equal pay for equal work (Randall 1982:183). After consultation with the CBI and TUC, it was agreed that the act passed in 1970 would take effect in 1975. Randall (ibid., 184) attributes the support of the TUC for equal pay legislation not to its concern for feminism but to its fear that lower women's wages would undercut those of men. Lorwin and Boston (1984:146) point out that until the late 1960s, unions preferred to deal with matters of equal pay through wage negotiations rather than through the legislative process. (Swedish unions, in a similar manner, opposed equal opportunities legislation in the 1970s.)

The EPA provided that machinery for complaints would be the same as that for other industrial disputes: efforts to reach a settlement via the Advisory Conciliation and Arbitration Service (ACAS), recourse to industrial tribunals, and, as a last resort, employee appeals tribunals. The passage of the act did not end the demand for sex discrimination legislation. Private member's bills were introduced after 1967 by Joyce Butler. A 1972 bill introduced by Willie Hamilton provided the basis for a bill placed by Baroness Nancy Seear before the House of Lords. It was then referred to a Select Committee; a similar Select Committee was es-

tablished in the House of Commons. The Conservative
Party then in power announced support for an equal opportunities commission and some form of legislation
(Randall 1982:164; Rendel 1978). The ensuing Labour
government in 1974 pledged support for strong sex discrimination legislation. The SDA was passed in 1975,
providing for expanded scope and enforcement and a
more powerful EOC.

The legislative process involved in the sex discrimination bill suggests that there was little opposition to
the idea of some kind of legislative action on the issue.
"The most admirable feature of the debate was the generally sympathetic attitude of the opposition," at least
as far as the principle of the bill was concerned; the bill
survived the parliamentary legislative process virtually
intact (Byrne and Lovenduski 1978b:137). It may be argued that activity of women in the two major parties
created both a pressure and political climate in which
legislation was thought necessary. However, there was,
in fact, little influence by feminists or female politicians
in Parliament (Jenson 1982:365). The Labour government in power in 1974 did endorse the idea of an enforcement body with strong powers as opposed to an organization that, as envisioned by the Conservatives,
would be largely devoted to campaigning. Among parliamentary groups, the NCCL, the TUC, the Fawcett Society, and Women in the Media, as well as a short-lived
Women's Lobby, pressed avidly for legislation. At the
other extreme, the act's passage was greeted with total
hostility by segments of the feminist community, who
described it as "fraudulent," "hypocrisy," "a sellout,"
and "miserable tokenism" and conducted a National
Day of Action against the bill, chaining themselves to the
railings outside Parliament (Bouchier 1984:120). Their

opposition was based on the loopholes in the act, its presumed middle-class bias, and the weakness of the EOC. They viewed the SDA as a cheap concession, aimed at staving off more meaningful and expensive demands for economic and family equality (ibid., 121). In the end, however, it appears that "lobbying was relatively weak and what mattered was M.P.s' willingness to pay [the bill] attention" (Randall 1982:184). As was the case with equal credit legislation in the United States, M.P.'s may have perceived the bill's proposals as a bow to a growing "women's vote," somewhat in anticipation of organized demands (Gelb and Palley 1987). Other reasons for the easy passage were Britain's pending entry into the Common Market—and the EEC directives requiring equal pay and job equality—and, as in the United States, the relationship between action against race discrimination and action against sex discrimination (Randall 1982:185; Meehan 1985:82).

A third law, the Employment Protection Act of 1975, was supported vigorously by the TUC (Lorwin and Boston 1984:147). The act gave women, for the first time, statutory protection against the loss of jobs due to pregnancy and childbirth. Women now had a statutory right to paid maternity leave, protection from unfair dismissal during pregnancy, and the right to regain their jobs up to 29 weeks of giving birth (Coote and Campbell 1987:93–94). However, in practice, the rights defined are so narrow that only a minority of women qualify; the majority cannot meet criteria regarding length of service and hours worked per week. No more than one woman in ten who leaves work to have a baby returns (Bruegel 1983:153). Only some 5 percent of women in manual work who took maternity leave and wished to return to their job have been able to do so (ibid.).

The record nonetheless demonstrates that the 1970s

in Britain marked legislative acceptance of the principle of equality in several different areas. How well has the legislation worked in practice?

We have suggested that the role of women's groups in facilitating the passage of legislation was an auxiliary rather than central one. Their participation has been even more minimal in the implementation process. As suggested earlier in this chapter, the EOC, which was set up under the Sex Discrimination Act, has been limited in its role, and, reflecting the systemic constraints within which it operates, has acted cautiously. Neither unions nor feminist groups have pressured vigorously for increased action, either at the EOC or in places of employment (Glucklich 1984:113). The EOC has used its power of formal investigation and its power to issue nondiscrimination notices "judiciously." In 1979 it issued its first (and only) nondiscrimination notice (ten have been issued by the Commission on Racial Equality) on equal pay to the Electrolux factory at Luton (*Spare Rib*, Sept. 1979:23). A lawsuit involving "indirect" discrimination (i.e., qualifying conditions were more often met by men than women) was successfully won in *Price v. Civil Service*. The SDA leaves untouched existing protective labor legislation, except to require the EOC to report on it (Bruegel 1983:152). Hedged with "genuine occupation qualifications" based on sexual distinctions, it fails to provide any obligation to establish positive (affirmative) action programs (ibid.). It is difficult to escape the view that the EOC was not given adequate legal machinery to enforce nondiscrimination on any significant scale (Lorwin and Boston 1984:150). And, as suggested earlier, the EOC has been cautious about using those powers it does have, preferring to devote its major resources to research and publicity.

In the British system, the individual is responsible for

bringing cases before the appropriate authorities, and there is the assumption of an equal balance of power between the employee and employer. The onus is on the woman to prove that discrimination has occurred. There is no right to obtain all documentation related to the case for the complaint. And individuals who can prove they have been discriminated against can obtain financial compensation but cannot regain their jobs (Ruggie 1984:118). The burden of proof is on the victim. Since 1976, between 50 and 70 percent of EPA and SDA cases have failed to reach a tribunal. This situation has been largely due to the intervention of the Advisory Conciliation and Arbitration Service, which, as the conciliation service for all industrial complaints, may intervene when there is a prospect of success or when either side requests its assistance. The majority of cases are "settled" at this level or withdrawn (Atkins and Hoggett 1984:28, 123).

The number of cases heard and upheld under both acts is discouraging to feminist aspirations. In recent years the number of cases brought to the EOC under the SDA has remained at a relatively low 250 annually, but EPA cases dropped from 1,742 in 1976 to 54 in 1981, which indicates that the EPA in particular has had limited impact (*Guardian*, June 16, 1982) (see Table 5) because women have become disillusioned with its ability to change their economic circumstances.

In most instances, under the SDA only a handful of cases heard by tribunals result in a positive finding for women. Of the cases that are conciliated, most are "settled," often for token sums, while a large and puzzling number are withdrawn with no settlement (*Spare Rib*, Sept. 1979:22; Ruggie 1984:123). The number of applications, never high, has almost steadily fallen, and

Table 5.
Industrial Tribunal Statistics, 1976–81,
on Equal Pay Act and Sex Discrimination Act

Applications to Tribunals Where Action Has Been Completed

Year	EPA	SDA	Total
1976	1,742	243	1,985
1977	751	229	980
1978	343	171	514
1979	263	178	441
1980	91	180	271
1981	54	256	310

Outcome of Cases Heard

1981		
Total heard	50.0	34.8
Dismissed	38.9	28.5
Upheld	11.1	6.3
1980		
Total heard	28.6	38.3
Dismissed	24.2	30.6
Upheld	4.4	7.8

SOURCE: Equal Opportunities Commission 1982: Appendix 3, p. 32.

from 1977 to 1978 almost one-third of the applicants were men (*Spare Rib,* Sept. 1979:22).

Amendments to the EPA and SDA might strengthen their significance by clarifying the meaning of "work of equal value," allowing for greater use of "positive action," and permitting the institution of class action suits. Such amendments are supported both by the EOC and the TUC Women's Advisory Committee (Ruggie 1984: 130). Efforts to reformulate the legislation have also been endorsed by the EEC. In 1982, the European Court of Justice struck down the EPA, saying that Britain has failed to broaden its definition of equal work to conform with the EOC's requirement of equal pay for work of equal value. When the Conservative government declined to comply with the ruling, Jo Richardson in 1983 introduced a private member's Sex Equality Bill, which would extend the definition of equal pay and bring under its aegis the growing number of female part-time workers (Perrigo 1985:138). The bill was defeated, but it could serve as a model for future legislation if a Labour-led government in conjunction with feminist campaigners pressed for its passage at a later time. As noted earlier, in 1984, after nine years, the government finally complied with the 1975 EEC directive that mandated equal pay for equal value. The ensuing amendment to the EPA resulted in several hundred new complaints over the next two years.

By 1980 a new Employment Act had eroded the maternity rights awarded to women in 1975. The act qualifies the right to maternity leave by limiting it to women who work 16 or more hours and have had two years of continuous service with their firm. Part-time workers rights are qualified even more. The size of the firm is now also taken into account in the act; exemptions are given to firms with fewer than six employees. Notification requirements of intent to return to work are made more stringent. Finally, employers are no longer required to provide identical work to returning employees; rather they may offer "suitable alternative work" (*Spare Rib*, June 1981:9). The act also makes it more difficult for women to claim unfair dismissal.

Under these circumstances, the implementation of equality acts and subsequent legislative process have undoubtedly been a distinct disappointment to women's aspirations. In the absence of a sympathetic judiciary, committed at least in principle to equal rights, and of a government agency with strong powers devoted to anti-discrimination concerns, much of the legislation enacted remains inadequate. Feminist campaigning groups such as the ROW, the NCCL, and the Women's Liberation Campaign for Financial and Legal Independence have pressed for legislative change and the extension of principles of equality in terms of focus (e.g., positive, or affirmative, action) and scope (e.g., extension to social security and tax law). Nonetheless, it is difficult to disagree with the view that "only the organization of women for women" can help reverse existing labor market inequalities (Meehan 1983a : 103). This course would involve the creation of policy networks, at this time lacking in the fragmented feminist political culture of Britain.

What of legislation dealing with social and moral issues? Cases in point are abortion reform and policies toward battered women. Abortion reform was brought before Parliament as a private member's bill, although lobbying by the Abortion Law Reform Association (ALRA) was important in gaining the bill's passage. Pym and others (Pym 1974:91; Rivers 1974:206) have argued that this is one of the few instances in which a promotional group has successfully "penetrated" the legislative process. Marsh and Chambers (1981:1) also contend that "interest group activity on abortion is un-paralleled. There are more interest groups concerned with this topic and they are more politicized than on any other social issue." Randall (1982:183–85) con-cludes that, as in the case of sex discrimination legisla-tion, developments within Parliament were crucial in facilitating the measure's passage. Again, the House of Lords played a key role when Lord Silkins' bill provided an important precedent. In the House of Commons, the sympathetic Labour government gave the bill extra time, while the pro-abortion vote on a Third Reading came primarily from a Labour majority that was re- form oriented, young, and middle-class (other moral re- form issues that gained support during this period were eased divorce and censorship rules, abolition of the death penalty, and legislation decriminalizing homo- sexuality) (Marsh and Chambers 1981:3).

Because the issue was "unwhipped," it reflected some- thing other than a straight "party" vote. At the same time there was a strong relationship between Labour Party membership and a pro-abortion vote. (In the United States, similar trends regarding abortion are evident in the stance of liberals and conservatives and in congressional voting [Gelb and Palley 1987:138]). David Steel, who introduced the bill, proved an able parliamentarian who consulted widely and made con- cessions to the medical profession to gain support (Marsh and Chambers 1981:19). Opposition forces were not well organized, while the "benevolent neutrality" of the Labour Government supported the reform effort (ibid., 20).

The act that was finally passed authorized abortion up to 28 weeks of pregnancy in cases where two regis- tered doctors agreed that the life of the mother or other children would be at risk, or that the baby was likely to be born handicapped. At the time of passage, numerous feminists opposed the act as inadequate because it failed to establish the principle of "abortion on demand," and they decried the definition of abortion as a medical rather than a woman's right. However, since the act's passage, the women's movement has been actively involved in efforts to defend it against restrictive provisions and limitations of its scope (Jenson 1982:356; Perrigo 1985:134).

In the aftermath of the act's passage in 1967, as in the United States after the 1973 Supreme Court decision legalizing abortion, groups formed either to oppose or preserve the legislation. These efforts have been described as "a near classic case of parliamentary lobbying—possibly unrivalled in the post-war era" (Marsh and Chambers 1981:40). By the mid-1970s, ALRA had been more or less eclipsed by the National Abortion Campaign (NAC), the women's liberation group described in Chapter 2. NAC was less committed to parliamentary lobbying than to politicizing public opinion on abortion-related issues. Its strategy was largely extraparliamentary, emphasizing proselytizing through demonstrations and picketing (ibid., 47). As radical socialist feminists, NAC members also maintained close ties with the Labour Party and trade unions. This relationship produced TUC support for defeat of the antiabortion Corrie Bill in 1979. In March 1981, NAC and other groups were surprised when, in the absence of parliamentary debates, the DHSS issued new forms concerning abortion that contained no nonmedical grounds for termination of pregnancy (Kingdom 1985:148). NAC and other groups have thus far been able to prevent any prosecutions for noncompliance with this administrative edict. In 1981 as well, a bill to make NHS facilities mandatory for abortion was introduced in Parliament, failing by 215 to 139 votes, but nonetheless indicating considerable support for this initiative (Randall 1982:174). An important factor in stopping antichoice restrictions was the Coordinating Committee in Defense of the 1967 Abortion Act (Co-Ord), founded in 1976. By 1980, with 50 member organizations, this unique organization had developed a strong defensive posture, unifying such diverse groups as ALRA, medical groups, unions, and the Labour Abortion Rights Campaign (LARC) (Marsh and Chambers 1981:48, 53). Labour Party women, including M.P.'s Jo Richardson and Oonagh McDonald as well as Chief Women's Officer Joyce Gould, helped greatly in defending abortion reform in Parliament. Vallance (1979:75) argues that abortion reform produced a rare example of collective action by Labour women in the House (although some Labour women—for example, Shirley Williams, a Catholic—opposed the measure). In addition, opposition forces were not well organized. The anti-abortion movement in the United Kingdom has lacked unity and mass support, in contrast to the strong pro-abortion organization in Parliament coordinated with extraparliamentary forces.

As in the United States, the feminist viewpoint has been incorporated in the liberal perspective (Marsh and Chambers 1981:94). Nonetheless, party affiliation is a better predictor of abortion policy-making in Britain, and because of the importance of Parliament in decision-making on this issue, attention has focused on that body. In the United States many more levels of government have been involved in abortion policy-making, including the courts, whose role has been central, as well as state and even urban legislative bodies.

A final case of women-related social legislation to be considered is policy toward battered women. The concept of state aid and public concern for battered women originated in the United Kingdom in 1972. By 1975, the National Women's Aid Federation (NWAF) had been formed to act as a communications and support net-work. In 1976, the Domestic Violence and Matrimonial Proceedings Act was passed in Parliament. As in the case of abortion, it was introduced as a private member's bill by Labourite Jo Richardson and enjoyed (some) sup-port from the Labour government (Coote and Gill 1979). The NWAF and the NCCL aided in building support for the act's passage. The issue was first raised during deliberations by a Select Committee in the House of Commons (as in the case of other women-related legisla-tion), at which testimony was presented by women's aid organizers and women victims of domestic violence. The committee found existing criminal and civil laws weak and recommended change. (As in the United States, po-lice had frequently refused to intervene in what the state viewed as "domestic disputes," and appropriate legal remedies were often not available.) The act that was passed in 1976 (and put into effect in 1977) was a modest effort that sought to strengthen procedures by which a woman could obtain a court injunction to re-strain a violent husband or cohabitee.

The 1976 act offers valuable protection in the county courts, permitting exclusion and nonmolestation in-junctions without recourse to other judicial proceedings (McCann 1985:74–75). The 1978 Domestic Proceedings and Magistrates Court Act extended similar protection to that which existed in county courts, but for married women only. The 1977 Housing (Homeless Persons) Act obliged local authorities to provide abused women with alternative accommodations.

However, according to McCann and others (ibid.; Hanmer 1977:101), since the enactment of the new laws, the judiciary has favored a limited interpretation of them, largely returning the position of abused wives to their pre-1976 role. The police response has indicated a similar reluctance to utilize the powers inherent in the new legislation. Funding, criminal justice reform, and therapy for victims of violence play a lesser role in the United Kingdom than the United States (Dobash and Dobash 1984:177).

There is absolute discretion with regard to a "power of arrest" attached to injunctions; the Home Office has limited powers of arrest to only three months (Rogers 1983:142). No national government funds have been committed thus far to provide financial aid for shelters or victim's related costs; local refuges are funded by local authorities.

Although Women's Aid has never seen legislation as particularly important in altering power relations between men and women (ibid., 146), the group did campaign not only for the 1976 act but also for the Housing Act of 1977, which gave priority to women and children for access to housing if they left home because of violence.

This brief survey of legislative enactments pertaining to feminist concerns leads to the conclusion that feminists have been able to influence public policy primarily as an auxiliary resource for parliamentary actors who are responsible for initiating and passing the legislation. As our analysis has demonstrated, most legislation in the United Kingdom came about through pressure, not from feminists, but rather from parties and unions, frequently through the vehicle of private members' bills in Parliament and often with considerable support in the House of Lords.

As we have indicated, legislative support for measures involving women's equality and welfare has left parties and unions free to pursue issues of equality in the workplace and in their own decision-making bodies at their own (snail's) pace and on their own terms, leaving basic structures of power and male dominance largely untouched (Scott 1982:180). Further, it appears that in Britain implementation of policies enacted regarding equal rights has often been more difficult to secure than the legislation itself. Given the nature of the administrative process outlined earlier, there is virtually no mechanism for interested groups to ensure compliance with enacted policy. This analysis suggests that the impact of policy aimed at women's concerns in Britain has been less than impressive, while at the same time legislation may serve as a convenient symbol muting further demands for political change.

The United States

In the United States an Equal Pay Act was enacted in 1963, with little conflict. As suggested earlier, after the Civil Rights Act of 1964, other women's rights legislation was passed with greater input from feminist groups. In addition, in the implementation process, feminist groups have been vigorous, often acting to strengthen legislation through administrative intervention or judicial proceedings.

Easy passage of legislation on equal rights in regard to education and credit in the 1970s may be attributed to the presence of a policy network in Washington after the ERA. Coalitions of women's groups specialized for specific policy areas lobbied both behind the scenes and overtly to promote legislative efforts and prevent the erosion of legislative gains once secured (Gelb and Palley 1987:53–56). The absence of strong party input on equal rights issues and the vulnerability of representatives to pressure from organized constituents created an atmosphere different from that in the United Kingdom. In addition, as we pointed out earlier, the politicization of the bureaucracy led to continued activity by organized feminist groups and their allies at the administrative level to ensure continued commitment to statutory aims.

To a greater degree than in Britain, feminists have continued to present legislative initiatives even during the 1980s, in a less hospitable political atmosphere, achieving some degree of success with portions of the Economic Equity Act. In Britain, efforts to interact with the political process have been more defensive and reactive.

As in Britain, the activity of grass-roots groups engendered a changed public consciousness regarding domestic violence, the result being the creation of over 700 local shelters. But unlike the case in Britain, grass-roots women "forged alliances with Congress, the administration and national women's organizations" (Zeitlin 1983 : 266). Although federal legislation was initially defeated and finally resulted in only modest funding, the effort to pass a federal law generated the coalescence of a new policy network. And although federal legislation fell short of feminist goals, in several important ways the movement to gain public support for the policy area succeeded. First, although it was short-lived, a federal agency, the Office on Domestic Violence (ODV), was created in the Department of Health, Education and Welfare during the Carter administration, and it helped focus attention on wife abuse as a serious political concern. Second, federally based lobbying efforts galvanized the movement against domestic violence. Third, legislation was passed at the state and local levels that provided, as in Britain, for increased responsiveness by the legal process, but, in addition, other policy initiatives were undertaken that increased support for victims of domestic violence.

In 1977, in the wake of the 1975 establishment of NOW, hundreds of interested representatives from all over the country attended a meeting of the Task Force on Domestic Violence in Milwaukee. This gathering led to the creation of a new group, the National Coalition Against Domestic Violence (NCADV), which began to mobilize on a national basis and press for legislation. The issue was further highlighted by the International Women's Year convention in 1977 and by hearings conducted by the U.S. Commission on Civil Rights. In response to pressure from feminist groups, the Carter administration created the ODV, with the mission of disseminating information and funding technical assistance and demonstration projects. Another federal agency, the Law Enforcement Assistance Program (LEAA), had been supporting and funding direct service and mediation programs for domestic violence victims since the mid-1970s.

In 1977, legislation to combat domestic violence was introduced in Congress. Female members of Congress, as well as such congressmen as Democrat George Miller of California, endorsed federal funding of community-based shelters (Gelb 1983:255). The bill failed to pass in 1978 largely because of concern over procedural issues in the legislative process. Further objections were raised, as they would be with increasing frequency, to the concept of federal intervention in domestic life and the creation of yet another federal social program. The bill was reintroduced the following year, in the 96th Congress, with support from an extremely broad coalition of supporters, including feminist and traditional women's groups, the police, prosecutors, religious groups, the National Football League, and the Junior League (Zeitlin 1983:271). By this time, the NCADV had established headquarters in the capital and comprised some 350 groups and 25 state coalitions. Although the group had developed a national lobbying presence, it continued to support the concept of community control of shelters by affected women in accordance with feminist principles of participatory democracy. Support for the bill was also forthcoming from female members of the congressional staff and feminists in the bureaucracy, particularly from the ODV and a large number of co-sponsors in Congress itself.

The bill passed the House by a vote of 292 to 106, with all congresswomen voting in favor of it—a key reason for the victory being "the work both by the sponsors with their colleagues and by shelter providers and other groups in their home districts" (Gelb, J., 1983:258). As passed, the bill would have provided for $65 million over a three-year period to supply "seed money" for local shelters. A similar bill was approved in the Senate, but by this time it had become the object of a concerted attack by right-wing forces. The bill passed the Senate narrowly, and a House-Senate Conference Committee was convened to resolve the differences in the two bills. The conference report passed the House easily, but a massive lobbying campaign by the "New Right" continued to oppose the bill's passage in the Senate. The Senate did not take up the bill until after the election of 1980, when a major shift in power took place. Under threat of a filibuster, and lacking sufficient votes to invoke cloture, the bill was never brought to the floor again and died. The failure of the legislation to pass meant the death of the ODV as well, although some of its functions were merged into the National Center on Child Abuse and Neglect.

This significant defeat at the national level was accompanied by numerous cutbacks in federal aid to victim-related programs. In 1984, Congress appropriated $6 million for shelter funding, in a more modest version of earlier legislation (and a far cry from the defeated bill's proposal of $65 million over a three-year period). In subsequent years such funding has continued, and several additional federal programs now also provide support for victims of wife battering.

Given the nature of the federal system, however, prospects for change at the state level have appeared much brighter. In recent years three-quarters of the states have altered their policies regarding battered women, usually providing some funding for shelters and improved access to a more responsive legal system (ibid., 251). By 1981, 49 states and the District of Columbia had passed some form of reform legislation to combat domestic violence (*New York Times*, Jan. 27, 1986: A13). Most states have created new civil and criminal remedies for abused victims. States and numerous cities have specified in detail the duties of police who respond to domestic violence calls, mandated better recordkeeping, and often created special training programs for police and judicial personnel. Police departments in more and more cities yearly report an increasing number of arrests for domestic violence (Gelb, J., 1983: 250–51).

In addition, and most importantly in the short run, states have provided funds for shelters and other victim-related services, including job training, child care, and legal and psychological counseling for abused women (Temkin 1986: 26–29). Some states have raised additional revenue for their programs through surcharges on marriage licenses and divorce filing papers. Significantly, the policies leading to such improvements have been promoted largely under the aegis of state coalitions against domestic violence, which have lobbied for change in conjunction with a wide group of coalition supporters and carefully cultivated legislative support. These groups have continued to monitor the implementation of policies after their passage. It seems accurate to conclude that in the United States the scope and significance of legislation on domestic violence has been greater than in Britain, largely owing to the existence of a feminist lobby and a newly created policy network focusing on wife abuse.

While in both countries the grass-roots orientation of the battered-women issue has been maintained, resources have been more readily available in the United States, thanks to lobbying and legislative pressure. Even grass-roots American activists have moved in the direction of coalitions (often via state coalitions against domestic violence), greater organizational strength, and more avowed politicization than their British counterparts.

A similar point is made by Jennifer Temkin (ibid., 38–39) in her analysis of law reform for rape in Britain and the United States. American women's groups lobbied tirelessly for reform and developed liaisons with media representatives and politicians of all political persuasions. They engendered public interest and support through newsletters and other efforts, creating laws that resulted in a larger number of arrests and convictions in cases of sexual assault and improving the treatment of victims within the legal process. In contrast, similarly radical law reform in Britain "in the mid-1980's . . . is as remote a prospect as ever" (ibid.).

In the absence of a cohesive and powerful women's lobby, as well as the general absence of women from corridors of power, recommendations by the House of Lords were modified to permit judges to consider the victim's sexual history and to extend efforts to gain anonymity for the victim and for the defendant as well. A 1984 Criminal Law Revision Committee similarly permitted rape to be viewed within a narrow perspective (Edgell and Duke 1983), providing for little change, particularly in comparison with U.S. legislation.

Political Opposition to Feminism in the United States and Britain

In both the United States and Britain the past decade has seen the ascendancy of conservative political administrations that have sought to reprivatize political issues, particularly those affecting the family and dependent women. There can be little doubt that the policies articulated by both British and American conservatives have a disproportionately negative policy impact, both on public sector employment and on availability of necessary public services especially important for dependent women (Lewis 1983:11). To what degree does the emergence of a New Right suggest negative future outcomes for feminist aspirations?

Recent politics in both countries have been marked by attacks on the role of the state in the economy and by the reassertion of traditional values regarding the family and the role of women (Conover and Gray 1984:91). In the United States some of the same forces that led to the emergence of feminism as a social movement have led to its antithesis, the New Right and the anti-abortion "pro-family" movement. Galvanized in part

by the Supreme Court decision in *Roe v. Wade,* which
helped create one sector of the feminist movement, anti-
feminists mobilized to oppose the ruling. They have
viewed the expansion of government activism as threatening to traditional values and have organized effectively to combat what they regard as pernicious social
tendencies. Aided by reforms in campaign financing
(leading to an extraordinary growth in Political Action
Committees [PACs]) and the relative decline in political
parties, they have organized effectively to lobby at the
congressional and administrative level and to seek to
achieve change via the electoral process.

The New Right has been extremely adept at using direct mail to raise large sums of money, at grass-roots
lobbying and indirect lobbying, and at influencing politics primarily through efforts to affect the outcomes of
elections (Lewis 1983:14). In the United States, one arm
of the New Right has linked antifeminism to a religious
base (the Catholic Church and fundamentalist religious
groups), which has provided powerful support for religious conservatives. The other arm includes such
groups as Phyllis Schlafly's Eagle Forum, dedicated to
restoring women to their traditional role in the family
and in society, and the anti-abortion "Right to Life"
movement. These forces were able to converge effectively with the Reaganite Republican Party in the 1970s
and 1980s, gaining a significant role both in the party
and in the Reagan administration.

It is probable that one source of the greater opposition to U.S. than to British feminism is the American
women's movement's greater visibility and impact.
Hence, antifeminism may constitute a larger segment of
New Right politics in this country, although at the same
time it remains only one interest group within the cur-

rent Republican orbit. Other groups include some elements of the eastern establishment, cold warriors, and economic conservatives. The somewhat uneasy coalition erected during Reagan's reign may prove to be too fragile to endure. It appears, however, that in the United States both the women's movement and the New Right are strong (Light and Lake 1985), and it is by no means clear that feminism has been routed. Support for Reagan's personal leadership has apparently not meant a significant shift to the right among the American public; rather, judgments about Reagan's leadership qualities and personality and about the state of the economy appear to have been most significant in aiding his electoral victories (Conover and Gray 1984:16). Nor have candidates backed by the right wing continued to sustain the electoral momentum they seemingly had in the late seventies and early eighties.

There is little evidence that the election of either 1980 or 1984 constituted a conservative mandate or that the two major symbolic issues of the New Right—abortion and the ERA—had any impact on the outcome of the vote (ibid., 15). Nor does it appear that the outcomes of most House and Senate races are attributable to New Right efforts. The power of this new coalition in shaping mass attitudes and political behavior does not seem particularly great. Nor has public opinion regarding abortion and the ERA shifted to the right (ibid., 158). Single-issue voting by members of the New Right does not seem to have a major impact on outcomes either (Ferguson and Rogers 1986:45–46).

Regarding abortion, for example, an NBC News exit poll in 1984 found that two-thirds of the electorate endorsed the legalization of abortion, with the decision "left to the woman and her physician," while only a quarter did not. Soon after the election, an ABC News poll found the share of Americans supporting the relatively radical position that women should have a right to abortion on demand, "no matter what the reason," actually increased over Reagan's first term, rising from 40 percent in 1981 to 52 percent in 1985, while the percentage opposing abortion on demand declined from 59 to 46 percent. According to a *Los Angeles Times* poll, only 23 percent of the electorate supported a constitutional amendment prohibiting abortion, and only 32 percent of those who voted for Reagan endorsed his policy on abortion. Louis Harris reports that Americans support passage of the ERA by 60 to 34 percent. And few Americans are enthusiastic about Jerry Falwell, the most prominent leader of the religious right. A 1984 *Los Angeles Times* exit poll found that only 16 percent of the voters approved of the minister (ibid.).

Recent trends in public attitudes toward affirmative action merit special notice because of the Reagan administration's sustained attack on affirmative action and repeated insistence on the public's impatience with such "special interests" as women and minorities. In 1978, Louis Harris reported that only 45 percent of the public agreed that "if there are no affirmative action programs helping women and minorities in employment and education, then these groups will continue to fail to get their share of jobs and higher education, thereby continuing past discrimination in the future"; 36 percent disagreed. By September of 1985, 71 percent agreed and 27 percent disagreed. Those favoring a "federal law requiring affirmative action programs for women and minorities in employment and education, provided there are no rigid quotas," numbered 67 percent by 1984, and those opposed, 18 percent; by 1985, support had risen to 75 percent (opposition was 21 percent). Here, too, the trends in public opinion have been directly opposite to the trends in public policy.

Partially as a consequence of Reagan's failure to extend his coattails to other offices, primarily in Congress, his strategy has been to seek only marginal policy changes, regardless of his rhetoric. This approach has tended to moderate the impact of New Right forces on the actual policy process, as compromise and incrementalism dominate the need to operate in the practical world. The prospects for continued Republican ascendancy rely far more on economics than on the conservative social agenda, which lacks broad public support and even endorsement from many coalition members (Jacobson 1985:232–33). Although right-wing activism has had a major impact on administrative appointments and consequently on policymakers as well, the long-term effects on policy remain unclear. What is clear is that while feminists have been forced into a more defensive political role, and subject to considerable harassment in the legislative and administrative process, they have not been totally defeated. The fragmentation of American politics, both at the federal level and in state and local initiatives, as well as the degree to which feminism has been institutionalized as a legitimate interest group continuing to intervene effectively in policy-making, would suggest that all is not lost.

Examining the organization and mobilization of the pro-family movement versus the feminist movement, Conover and Gray (1984:176) found that the feminist network is far better organized at the state level, having almost twice as many organized groups as the right in the 40 states they surveyed. In general, their analysis suggests that the significance of right wing organizational power is far less than the media and New Right itself would lead one to believe, although in terms of financial resources they are formidable adversaries (ibid., 203–5).

In the United Kingdom, while similar shifts in the postwar consensus regarding the scope and direction of the welfare state exist and have been epitomized in the Thatcher government, several differences appear significant. First, given the importance of the party structure in Britain, the Thatcher government may represent a more coherent and tough-minded partisan bloc than Reagan's somewhat uneasy coalition (David 1983:198). Some observers perceive in Mrs. Thatcher's approach a significant break with traditional conservatism as well as with social democracy—an approach that has transformed the nature of British policies (Gelb, N., 1983). There is considerable evidence that the British public, particularly the skilled working class, has swung somewhat to the right, but nonetheless what has been called "authoritarian populism" may not reflect a complete or even significant rejection of the welfare state in Britain (Butler and Kavanaugh 1984:293). Nevertheless, there is support for some privatization and greater individualism as well as resentment of taxation and waste (ibid.).

In British politics it is clear that support for the Conservative party manifesto means decreased spending, including reductions in funding for housing and education; cuts in some state benefits (e.g., maternity and unemployment) and abolition of others as well, including supplementary benefits; reduced levels of public service and reduced subsidies to those services; and the privatization of public assets, including council housing and some industry (Edgell and Duke 1983:358–59). Most of these policy areas directly affect women as employees and clients of the state. Both the electorate and popular ideology have shifted to the right regarding abortion, women's rights, and welfare (Robertson 1984: 293). However, results of a recent poll indicate that the overwhelming majority of British women view abortion as legitimate if the woman's health is endangered, if the child is likely to be born deformed, or if the woman is a rape victim. Abortion is opposed if the child is not wanted or if the woman wishes to abort because she is unmarried (Langford 1980:11).

Anti-abortion views, in the absence of a religious base, have never gained the same political resonance in Britain as in the United States. While Prime Minister Thatcher holds views hostile to women's liberation, including her insistence that women with children remain out of the work force and her policy of defunding such areas as child care and state aid to dependent women, her rhetoric is not specifically antifeminist. However, the concern of her government for family policy—particularly via the all-male family policy group that has taken over important cabinet functions (Rogers 1983:44), most notably in the absence of consultation with women's groups (even such traditional ones as the Women's Institutes and Townswomen's Guilds)—implies a tacit antagonism to feminist issues (ibid., 108).

In contrast to the situation in the United States, and perhaps because of difficulties encountered by all promotional groups in the political arena, neither the Society for the Unborn Child (SPUC) nor LIFE, another anti-abortion group, has ever been able to gain a foothold in the political arena. Pro-choice groups such as NAC have been more effective in establishing relationships with M.P.'s and mounting campaigns for popular support. SPUC lacks a connection comparable to that of anti-abortion groups in the United States with the Catholic Church, which in any event denounced a SPUC effort in 1983, saying that the "ends don't justify the means" (*New Statesman*, June 24, 1983:4). The church itself lacks the numbers and fervor of its American counterpart and seems less avowedly political, particularly with regard to the abortion issue. Rogers (1983:157) reports that wide differences exist between the M.P.'s of different parties on social policy, 83 percent of Labour M.P.'s favoring free child care and 86 percent of Conservatives favoring the view that women be obliged to care for their children. The partisan cast of views on feminism is obvious and points up the possibilities inherent in the election of a more sympathetic government.

Only a future general election will reveal whether the vacuum left by the disarray of left-wing politics, created by the internal disorder of the Labour Party, will be filled either by the SDP or by a reconstituted Labour Party, permitting a different political attitude toward women to prevail.

Assessment

We have examined the policy process in the United States and Britain to determine the relative impact of the feminist movement in each nation. In the United States, while administrative agencies such as the EEOC have not always been effective and their enforcement strength has varied with political commitment, they have played a significant role with regard to non-discrimination policies. The EEOC has benefited from the existence of a feminist policy network that has not only influenced both policy orientation and political appointments, but has also been instrumental in gaining substantial judicial and public endorsement of principles of affirmative action. Such a supportive network has been lacking in the United Kingdom, where the superficially comparable EOC has been isolated politically in the absence of political and material resources.

In Britain, policy has generally been initiated by private members, and, in the case of sex discrimination, prodded by the EEC. Feminists have played the role of secondary activists, given their ambivalence about political participation in national-level politics and their frequent lack of information regarding the policy process. The absence of policy networks, combined with the highly centralized and closed system described earlier, prevents any significant feminist presence in the implementation process. Nonetheless, we have seen that feminists have intervened successfully in collective action on the abortion issue, where they have continued to maintain a political presence and sustained a sometimes uneasy alliance with such groups as labor unions. Abortion-related efforts point the way to coalition building on other issues, although it is not clear whether similar congruence may be achieved on economic policies. American feminists have engaged in extensive lobbying, networking, and coalition building on a variety of policy issues at the state, local, and national levels of politics, even making some policy inroads during the conservative Reagan era.

New Right opposition to the type of social change represented by feminism has developed in both Britain and the United States, necessitating a reactive and defensive role for feminist groups, as well as lessening their ability to set political priorities. However, Mrs. Thatcher's third electoral victory and British public opinion data indicate an even more substantial right-wing shift in the United Kingdom than in the United States. Given the considerable political and ideological obstacles to feminist political mobilization addressed earlier, the persistence and reinforcement of Conservative Party strength do not augur well for feminist influence in British national politics.

5

Sweden: Feminism Without Feminists?

The analysis presented thus far suggests the following propositions regarding political change, based on our comparison of Britain and the United States:

1. The importance of opportunity structures in facilitating social movement development and growth
2. The actual and potential significance of autonomous political activity by women—independent of intermediation by other political institutions—in creating the groundwork for political change
3. The degree to which changes in women's and societal consciousness facilitate the development of both individual and policy changes
4. The degree to which the impact of policy regarding women, particularly involving implementation, depends on the existence of an autonomous, gender-based political force and network

It may be argued that to examine these propositions by using only two cases is not sufficient. Therefore, in this chapter we examine the case of Sweden to help us further illuminate the processes leading to political and social change.

The Swedish Political Opportunity Structure

Sweden has often been viewed as the nation in which equality has proceeded further than in any other Western country. Ruggie (1984:17) regards Sweden as the society in which the interests of women workers have been most nearly realized, while Adams and Winston (1969) portray the Swedish approach to the integration of working women into the labor force and political system as in many ways superior to the American approach. Baude (1979:171) has suggested that Sweden has witnessed the development of a new role identity for women. The purpose of this chapter, then, is to examine what has been achieved in Sweden, viewed within the context of the propositions outlined at the outset. What light does the Swedish experience shed on issues of autonomy, the sources of social change, and the impact of feminism as a social movement on political systems?

To a far greater degree than is true for either Britain or the United States, Swedish politics has been dominated by the primacy of party government and the continuity of power. In Sweden, "the individual legislator is elected as one among several representatives from multimember constituencies. He or she is nominated by the party and represents the party more than the special interests of the constituency. Cabinet ministries and administrative agencies are formally separated from each other. In reality, though, there is close cooperation on most matters of policy interpretation and implementation guidelines. Special interests in Sweden are thoroughly organized. They are represented not only on the main vehicles for Swedish policy formulation, the Royal Commissions, but also on the boards of administrative agencies" (Lundqvist 1980:182). Moreover, the courts have no balancing power vis-à-vis the executive or legislative branches of government. Private interest groups thus cannot use the courts as a means for challenging government policy. In short, the center of gravity in the Swedish polity lies in the cabinet.

The bureaucratic structure in Sweden may appear to be more susceptible to party and other political intervention, and possibilities for recruitment to a more open political system seem greater than is the case in Britain. Nonetheless, the political impact of corporatism (tripartism), or representation of the economic groups (largely employers and unions), again moderates the extent to which promotional groups may gain representation.

Swedish political parties dominate interest group mobilization and aggregation as well as policy-making to a significant degree. In the highly organized Swedish state, the public sector makes up almost two-thirds of the Gross National Product, and public sector employment involves about 40 percent of the working population.

The Swedish system is recognized as a consensual democracy, or a liberal democratic state characterized by a low level of opposition to the framework of rules and regulations for the resolution of conflict (Elder, Thomas, and Arter 1982:10). In such a system, groups tend to be absorbed by the corporatist state; alienated subgroups that resort to violence, protest, or even dissent are rare, as evidenced by the relatively low incidence of strikes (until recently) and the tradition of voluntary collective agreements between business and labor. The system's apparent openness to popular views is exemplified by the commissions of inquiry that circulate proposals for reform projects for comment from agencies and interest groups (ibid., 28). The Riksdag (unicameral parliament) is generally reactive in nature, with most of its business structured by the administration of the government. The effort to resolve conflict with a minimum of controversy is perhaps best typified by the office of the ombudsman to oversee the legality of state administration—an office that dates back to the early eighteenth century (ibid., 138)!

In Swedish politics a distinction is made between policy formulation and day-to-day administration. Ministers establish directives and policies to be executed by agencies. Heads of ministries are politically appointed, and the small ministries function as their staffs. The over 100 agencies are responsible to the government, not to the ministries (ibid., 114). A strong tradition of local government gives extensive powers of initiative and action to the municipal councils and to executive committees that govern at the community level.

Swedish politics is characterized by a high degree of continuity. The Social Democratic Party (SDP) has dominated politics for 40 years, relinquishing its hold only in 1976–82, when a nonsocialist coalition ruled. However, because the five parties that in the main compose the Swedish political system represent only a relatively modest transition from left to right, political compromise is usually possible regardless of electoral outcomes. Swedish politics is also distinguished by a high degree of organizational participation. Nonetheless, most such participation tends to be economically oriented (80 percent of the people belong to labor market–related institutions).

There is a relatively low level of political activism other than voting; day-to-day participation and communal activity are limited in a society that relies heavily on state intervention (Olsen 1982:162). (However, data offered by Sainsbury [1983] indicate a larger percentage of petition signers and demonstrators in Sweden than in other Western democracies in the 1970s.) Women are less participatory than men, although the 1970s saw increased activism in parties, unions, and the like among young women (ages 16–24) (Erikson and Aberg 1987; Eduards, Halsaa, and Skjeie 1985; Sainsbury 1983). Whether this trend has survived women's domestic responsibilities and continued into the 1980s is open to question. The society is highly institutionalized, providing limited space for different or extraparliamentary views. To the degree that women's groups exist in Sweden, they tend to be traditional rather than "liberationist" in their orientation (Eduards, Halsaa, and Skjeie 1985:135). In this political context, promotional groups play only a minor role, and feminism, or women's liberation, is viewed with suspicion by many political actors (Scott 1982:157). The society emphasizes consensus and the absence of conflict; extrapolitical activity beyond the parliamentary system and public sector is rarely mobilized effectively (one exception was the nuclear power controversy in the mid-1970s). As most observers agree that in Sweden everything is "already so established" that new and small groups may have difficulty gaining a hearing and access (Olsen 1982:225), it is not surprising that no significant feminist movement has developed.

The search for consensus emphasizes participatory values, but in fact opponents are encouraged to compromise and accept government ideas and limited participation in policy formulation (Kelman 1981:174). Public debate is far more limited than that in the United States;

the circle of participating groups is determined by the government. Policy formulation is conducted primarily via state commissions that include all parties and "relevant" interest groups; these commissions are the key to power and influence as the Riksdag has increasingly become relatively powerless (ibid., 261). Only a small proportion—16 percent—of the commission members responsible for policy formation are women (Eduards 1986:6).

Because of the emphasis on consensus, there is little room for alternative recommendations (Olsen 1982: 164). The Riksdag acts on legislation whose passage is already assured. Perhaps even more than in Britain, the parliament's primary legislative function appears to be debate, not decision-making. Informal contacts between governmental leaders and organizations are a vital part of the system; personal contacts between such leaders, who constitute a relatively small elite (numbering several hundred, and based in Stockholm), dominate policy-making (ibid., 261; Kelman 1981:258).

With regard to values and social change, however, Sweden is among the most "advanced" nations in the world. In 1976, one of every two marriages ended in divorce (ranking Sweden just slightly behind the United States, the world leader in broken marriages), and one-parent families were two of every nine, or 18 percent, double the figure in the United Kingdom (Popenoe 1985– 86; Scott 1982:70). Out-of-wedlock births are common (45 percent) and relatively unstigmatized because children of nonmarried parents have rights equal to those of all others. One-third of households involve a single person only (Popenoe 1986:10), and the percentage of nonmarried cohabitees is the highest in the world—21 percent in 1983 (ibid., 8; Eduards 1986:12), whereas it was only 2.5 percent in Britain.

The percentage of women in higher education is almost equal to that of men, in contrast to Britain (Ruggie 1986:24), although at the postgraduate level their numbers drop significantly (Equality Ministry 1985). Swedish women tend to refrain from long-term education choices, diminishing their career alternatives (Mellstrom and Sterner 1980).

Work-related norms appear strong for women and men: a survey conducted at the end of the 1970s revealed that only 10 percent of Swedish women preferred domesticity to a life combining work and home (Scott 1982:41). Labor force participation by women is extremely high—in 1980 it was about 80 percent (Ruggie 1986:35). Most Swedish women work part-time; only 23 percent of women worked continuously at full-time jobs from 1978 to 1980 (Qvist, Acker, and Lorwin 1984: 275). In addition, occupational sex segregation in Sweden is among the highest in the industrialized world. Sweden and Britain demonstrate the highest proportion of sex segregation in OECD countries—82 percent and 76 percent, respectively, of women are found in sex-segregated occupations as employees of the welfare state (Rein 1985:44).

The Swedish unemployment rate is comparatively low, for women as well as men (2.7 percent, whereas it is 9.6 percent in Britain) (Equality Ministry 1985:10). More than half of women are employed by the public sector, primarily in local communities, where they are concentrated in the health and social services (Rein 1985:42; Qvist, Acker, and Lorwin 1984:276). Since 90 percent of blue-collar workers and 75 percent of white-collar workers belong to labor unions, women have joined them as well.

Female membership in the Landsorganisationen (LO), Sweden's dominant (blue-collar) trade union, increased from 7 percent in 1945 to 40 percent in the 1980s, but, as in Britain and the United States, the growth in female labor union membership has come primarily in the white-collar sector. Hence, other unions, such as the Central Organization of Salaried Employees (TCO), which represents most salaried workers, and the Swedish Confederation of Professional Organizations (SACO/SR), which represents professional groups, have the largest female presence. Women currently comprise over half the membership of the TCO and 35 percent of the SACO/SR (Ruggie 1986:9; Qvist, Acker, and Lorwin 1984:18; Hernes and Hanninen-Salmelin 1985:123).

Data on full-time, year-round employees in Sweden demonstrate a higher ration of women's pay as a proportion of men's (80.5 percent) than in either Britain or the United States. Although Sylvia Hewlett (1986:99) has argued that Sweden is the country with the smallest male/female wage gap, the assertion is true only if the large number of part-time female workers in Sweden is ignored. The percentage of women employed part-time has increased steadily since 1968—from 42 to 52 percent of employed women (in contrast to 23 percent in the United States) (Sundstrom 1985:52). Because so many Swedish women work part-time, the high male/female wage ratio conveys less than meets the eye. While Swedish men receive 63 percent of the wages, women receive only 37 percent (Equality Ministry 1985:12). Pay differentials are not so great between the sexes at ages 20 to 24, but become accentuated thereafter, especially during the childbearing years for women. In 1980, the average income for men was almost twice that for women (*Women and Men in Sweden* 1985). Among women with young children (under seven), especially two or more, the proportion of women who work part-time is 60 percent. Similarly, among women 45 to 64 with no children under 17, the part-time rate is 58 percent (Sundstrom 1985). Only among women who are childless and under 44 does the part-time employment rate drop (to 25 percent). As in the United States and Britain, part-time work results not only in male/female wage discrepancies, but also in marginalized relations with trade unions, as well as lack of mobility and of access to bonuses, overtime pay, and other rewards.

Swedish women hold relatively few high positions, especially in the private sector, where in 1978 they held only 0.2 percent of top positions in management (whereas men held 7 percent), 3 percent of senior executive positions and less than 1 percent of the jobs in public authorities and companies. They held 4 percent of senior government posts (Equality Ministry 1985:20). Both the United States and Britain have a higher percentage of women in top executive positions than does Sweden (ibid., 20). (See Chapter 6 for further discussion of this issue.)

As is the case of Britain and the United States, the effects of recession in recent years have often fallen disproportionately on female workers, who are often public-sector employees with marginal jobs.

The Structure of Politics and Women

The history of policy regarding women in Sweden early demonstrated tendencies still present today, as is true for other nations. In the 1800s, women in Sweden gained the right to attend school, equal inheritance rights, and the right to conduct business in their own names (Adams and Winston 1980:113)—all in the absence of an organized movement. Similarly, the struggle for women's suffrage was tied to universal suffrage. A National Association for Women's Suffrage, comprised largely of Social Democratic women, existed but pursued its course with a minimum of protest. Subsequently, suffrage came to be included on the agenda of the major political parties, and the struggle was conducted primarily in them. In the main, feminism was incorporated into the structure of political parties, creating a relationship that still persists (ibid., 115–16).

As in Britain, women's unions were established in the late 1800s and early 1900s. In the 1930s and 1940s the female trade unions merged with newly created white-collar federations to form the TCO and the Swedish Confederation of Professional Organizations (SACO/SR) (Qvist, Acker, and Lorwin 1984:262).

Unlike the case in Britain or the United States, a women's liberation movement has existed in only a minimal way in Sweden. Although a relatively militant Group 8 was created in the 1960s, it has never developed into a strong and coherent feminist movement with major influence in Swedish politics. Most feminists were more concerned with class than with gender (Eduards 1981:224), and the struggle for women's liberation was conducted primarily within parties and other political institutions. Militant feminism was unacceptable in a consensus-oriented society. In Sweden, neither alternative political structures nor consciousness-raising for individuals—both so important in the development of the British and American movements—were ever viewed as significant except among a few activists (Adams and Winston 1980:38).

However, the women's liberation movement in Sweden ought not to be entirely discounted. Founded in

1968, Group 8 had about 1,000 members. It was responsible for creating a sense of political activism, especially
during the 1970s. Although feminism is generally viewed
as "un-Swedish," the activists did influence people's
attitudes through media coverage and the subsequent
hiring of feminist columnists and writers by the two
major newspapers, *Dagens Nyheter* and *Svenska Dagbladet*. The movement sponsored women's houses in several Swedish cities and operated on the basis of small
decentralized groups—never more than ten members
(interview, Sangregorio 1985). Although the Group 8
barely exists today, a magazine, *Kvinnobulletinen*, is
published monthly, with a circulation of 3,000 to 4,000
(ibid.).

In comparison with the situation in Britain and the
United States, cultural and theoretical feminism have
never become a strong force in Sweden, nor have new
approaches to service delivery for women, such as rape
crisis centers, ever gained adherents. Nonetheless, as
we shall see, there has been political activity regarding
rape and a movement to create shelters for female victims of domestic violence. Consider this interesting commentary on the current status of the women's liberation
movement: When this interviewer asked her numerous
interviewees about the existence of a women's center in
the Stockholm area, she was repeatedly told, "I think
there is one but I don't know where." In fact, a women's
center and bookstore/informational center, Kvinnocentrum, has existed in the center of Stockholm, operated
by two women, since 1975. Several other "women's
houses" in the Stockholm area combine shelters with
other feminist-oriented activities. But the most successful tend to be the least overtly "women's liberationist"

and are funded by the local municipality and dominant party organizations. Nonetheless, annually, on March 8, numerous women's groups come together to celebrate International Women's Day. A study in Orebro found that the ideas of the women's liberation movement have had an impact on local legislators by increasing the number of women politicians, making them aware of the importance of gender-based concerns, and helping them structure the content of political debate—if not the political agenda—in a more feminist way (Hedlund and van der Ros Schive 1984).

Another approach to feminism is demonstrated by the Fredrika Bremer League, a women's rights organization (or liberal feminist group) created in 1884. In 1985 it claimed a membership of 6,000 (down from a high of 9,000) in local chapters seeking to increase the representation of women in party leadership and public life as well as engaging in networking (interview, Olafsson 1986). The league played a particularly vigorous role during 1976–82 when Birgitta Wistrand, a forceful and dynamic leader, was its president.

Despite the relatively limited influence of the league, it has apparently seemed threatening to many Swedes, including ministers of government and LO leaders who accused Birgitta Wistrand of being too aggressive and working for the "wrong" type of woman (Scott 1982: 162). Other Swedes portray the league as "bourgeois" and "bluestocking," in an effort to pejoratively place it beyond the acceptable political pale. In Swedish, unlike American society and politics, individual change is viewed as less important than structural and societal change (ibid., 137).

Although traditional women's organizations "have demonstrated a higher level of activity vis-à-vis the authorities than the new women's movement," the 1981 disbanding of the Swedish National council of Women's Organizations suggests a relatively limited base of activities for such groups in Sweden. The council had only ten member groups during its existence, a smaller number than in any other Nordic country (Eduards, Halsaa, and Skjeie 1985:135; Dahlerup and Gulli 1985:14).

Parties and Unions

In examining the role of Swedish women in political parties and unions, it seems inescapable that they have been more effective working via the parties than working in the unions. Although the structure of women's activities within the parties differs and women's issues are undoubtedly not in the forefront of party leaders' concerns, both in the Social Democratic Party (primarily in the 1960s when the sex role debate was first aired in Sweden) and in the more centrist parties since then, women have achieved a degree of influence.

As in Britain, women's sections in the parties have usually played a secondary role. However, in Sweden all the major parties support increased women's representation (Eduards 1986: 4; Hedlund and van der Ros Schive 1984:27).

Table 6 shows that representation of women at various levels of party organization has grown dramatically (although least at the top decision-making level). Nonetheless, virtually all the women party leaders interviewed felt that the concerns of women are often ignored and viewed as secondary by male party leaders. Women leaders of the SDP perceived the Liberal and Center parties as more interested in women than their own, dominant party (interview, Peanberg, 1986). The

Table 6.
Representation of Women in Swedish Political Parties, 1982

Party	Members			Congress			Representative Assembly			Executive Board			Working Committee		
	Total	Women	%	Total	Women	%	Total	Women	%	Total	Women	%	Total	Women	%
Center	140,941	10,993	8	285	91	32	90	26	29	17	4	24	7	2	29
Liberal	47,556	21,535	45	220	95	43	—	—	—	27	12	44	19	7	38
Conservative	155,550	63,000	41	200	70	35*	96	22	23	30	9	30	8	2	25
Social Democratic	1,205,064	363,706	30	350	119	34*	—	—	—	27	8	30	10	3	30
Communist	17,793	6,714	38	313	112	36	—	—	—	35	2	34	—	2	29

SOURCE: Haavio-Mannila et al. 1985: Table 3.2, p. 45.
*Data for 1981.

LO, linked historically to the Social Democrats, was seen as having a far more important role in the party than the women's organization. The members of the VPK, though lacking a women's section, often express views most sympathetic to a feminist perspective, particularly as reflected in 1985 data (Holmberg 1986).

Dahlerup's objectives for women's party organizations include cooperation with corresponding parties abroad. Although that may be an important goal, we will expand this idea to include collaboration among domestic political parties. Greater cooperation among the women in the five major Swedish parties in national politics has been evident. In an innovative effort in 1979, women from these parties joined together to demand increased representation. Other efforts followed in the 1980s and discussions across party lines have continued (Eduards 1981:223). Such efforts at cross-party discussions have no parallel in the more divisive and ideological politics of Britain. Meetings have been held in the Riksdag, occasionally resulting in joint policy on issues relatively insignificant to the respective parties (e.g., cliterodectomy among immigrant women). Joint demonstrations have also been directed toward reforms related to women, sometimes generated via women's leagues within the parties themselves.

In the SDP the National Federation of Social Democratic women (SSKF), founded in the 1880s, played a crucial role in bringing the issue of sex equality to the fore in the 1960s (in the 1950s it was especially active in opposing nuclear weapons) (Dahlerup and Gulli 1985: 6). A study group formed in 1960 produced a set of policy proposals regarding day care and sex role equality that was later incorporated into the 1969 party programs. More recently, the SSKF has generated internal debate and formulated programs related to women's concerns. Particularly in the 1970s, Social Democratic women were prominent in raising issues concerning the future of nuclear power in Sweden. But, partly as a result of dissension among younger feminists, the membership of the SSKF fell from 68,000 in the 1960s to 45,000 in 1974 (Eduards 1981:221). The federation is affiliated to the party, giving it only consultative status (similar to the situation of the British women's sections described in Chapter 3). In the SDP, sexual equality is subordinated to (or seen within the context of) class equality (Scott 1982:61). Although the SDP has called for increased representation for women at all levels, neither abortion nor affirmative action has ever become an important policy issue (Kelman 1981: 29). The SDP has demonstrated an ability to suck up all new movements of opinion and incorporate them into the party apparatus, and feminism has been no exception (ibid., 28).

All parliamentary parties adhere to the 60/40 principle: neither sex is to have more than 60 percent nor less than 40 percent of representation within party ranks. Nonetheless, some parties have been especially active in recruiting and nominating women; since the 1970s the Center Party (CKF—the agrarian party) has consistently returned the most women to the Riksdag (except in 1985, when the Liberal Party had 39 percent women, the SDP 34 percent, and the Center Party 33 percent) (Eduards 1986:4–6).

The Center Party has the largest women's organization in Sweden, with a membership of almost 75,000 (interview, Soderstrom, 1986). (Organized in 1,691 branches, these women hold membership only in the women's section of the party.) When the former foreign minister, Karin Soder, was elected head of the party in 1986, she became the first woman president of a Swedish political party (she has now resigned owing to ill-ness). Members of the women's organization have seats on the Center board. Most recently, the group has advo-cated a policy requiring every nominating list to con-tain the names of women. In the last election, at least one-third of the districts complied.

In 1972, the Liberal Party (Folkpartiet, or People's Party) translated its concern for women's equality into a demand for greater female representation, requiring that a minimum of 40 percent women be on all district boards and in all party bodies. The Federation of Lib-eral Women, founded in 1936, has a membership of over 20,000 and has been most successful in gaining repre-sentation of women by setting a goal of at least 40 per-cent representation at all levels of the party (Colon 1981–82:26). As of 1986, this goal had all but been achieved, with 39 percent female representation in the Riksdag, 33 percent on the Stockholm City Council, and 38 per-cent at the county level (interview, Branting, 1986). The Left Party Communists (VPK) do not have a women's section but rather a women's committee, which issued a women's program in 1979 and whose members are sym-pathetic to women's liberation.

The Moderate (or Conservative) Party women's asso-ciation, established in 1920, has its own membership and its members are also members of the party. With a membership of 67,000, it has moved away from a previ-ous policy in which all women party members were au-tomatically members of the women's section (Eduards, Halsaa, and Skjeie 1986). According to party leaders, the new policy has led to an increase in membership (in-terview, Haglund, 1986). The representation of women within the party at all levels has reached about 30 per-cent, except at the top level of the working committee, where their numbers are few. Most of the women's sections of parties stress the training and recruitment of women as candidates, as well as the significance of women's issues, such as day care and family and labor market policy.

It appears that at least several of Dahlerup's five objectives of separate women's organizations in parties have been achieved in Swedish parties. Among these are activation of women, recruitment for top posts, and pursuance of women's policies within the party. Swedish parties, particularly in contrast to the British ones, have reacted relatively rapidly to women's demands for increased representation and can therefore be described as fairly democratic (Skard and Haavio-Mannila 1985: 43). Kerstin Peanberg (interview, 1986) of the Social Democratic Women's Federation, for example, feels strongly that in the absence of the federation, there would be no national day-care policy in Sweden. While some women's sections have few powers, several derive their own support from dues as well as relying on party support, thus providing a degree of autonomy. Women politicians have often, though not always, emerged from the women's sections. One study found, for example, that 40 percent of Swedish M.P.'s used the organizational channel provided by women's organizations to advance politically (Sainsbury 1985:21–22). Women say that issues they first brought up in the women's organization of a party are subsequently raised at meetings of the party itself. More than half the women who have become active party members have been drawn from women's party groupings. Particularly in Stockholm, women's party organizations have mobilized to fight prostitution and pornography.

Throughout the 1960s and 1970s, the Center Party was the most active recruiter of women councilors (Sinkkonen 1985:96), but in the 1980s local representation has been similar for all parties. Because the Conservative and Liberal parties had higher female membership than the dominant SDP in 1985, although they are smaller parties, doubt is cast on the conventional wisdom that leftist parties are necessarily more sympathetic to feminist concerns. As in the United Kingdom, women still tend to be nominated for marginal seats. However, the party list system gives women a greater opportunity to gain representation than the single-member district system, especially if women are placed high on the list.

Women in Sweden have gained an unusually high degree of representation in the political system. A tremendous increase in electoral representation occurred in the 1970s, and by 1985 women constituted 31 percent of the Riksdag (ibid., 67). At the county and municipal levels women's representation has also surged since 1970; they now make up over 33 percent of county councils (up from 15 percent) and 30 percent of municipal councils (up from 14 percent) (Eduards 1986). Women's representation in high governmental positions has climbed, too; since 1982 five women have served in the 21-member cabinet.

Nonetheless, women still remain relatively isolated from leadership positions in the Riksdag and, even more importantly, in the crucial administrative sector (ibid., 7–8; Qvist, Acker, and Lorwin 1984:278). Moreover, they tend to be concentrated in areas associated with women's traditional societal role. Women's participation in administrative policy-making echelons is low on public commissions, which prepare policies to present to the Riksdag and play a key decision-making role. In 1983–84 there were only 16.8 percent women on such commissions, although this represents a 10 percent increase from the early 1970s. At the policy-making administrative level, 10 percent of the high-level appointees were women (Eduards 1986:6, 7). Women appear to be absent from most leadership roles and their public visibility is often limited as well (Adams and Winston 1980:141). While 28 percent of standing committee memberships in the Riksdag, where the most important work tends to be done, are held by women, they are best represented in committees dealing with social welfare, insurance, and cultural affairs. Women are allotted fewer influential appointments and are particularly weak in nonelected bureaucratic roles. A recent report found that the higher up in the administrative hierarchy, the fewer women present (women held only 26 of 251 senior-rank positions in 1986) (Sinkkonen 1985:88; "Equality Between Men and Women" 1987). Even when women tend to be given responsibility in areas of traditional concerns such as education and social welfare policy, they tend to have peripheral rather than central decision-making positions (Eduards 1986:9). And, once in office, women in government have tended to support party loyalties rather than gender concerns, in keeping with the structure we have outlined. Female party leaders' attitudes resemble party dictates more than feminist views, diverging as much as or more than men's attitudes on women-related issues (Kelman 1984:19).

In local-level politics, which are particularly important in determining the scope and direction of funding priorities such as day care, city councilors who have nominal authority are less significant than the heads of administrative committees. (The local policy-making structure is a fourfold one, ranging from municipal council members to members of municipal executives, to members of local administrative committees, to heads of administrative committees [interview, Hedlund, 1986].) Women's representation on committees rose from 1 percent in 1971 to 5 percent in 1977, although the increase was largely in committees dealing with "reproductive" rather than "productive" sectors (i.e., health and education, culture, child care and social affairs rather than technical issues and economic questions) (Sinkkonen 1985:85–86).* Thus, the pattern of isolation from power in all but limited areas is reflected in local, as well as national, politics.

Unions

Given the corporatist approach that characterizes Swedish policy-making, unions occupy a particularly significant political role. As is true for parties, unions have put their support behind equality-oriented goals, although, as is the Swedish norm, such support is forthcoming in the absence of feminist demands or a special role for women's groups (Scott 1982:53). The Swedish "sex equality" ideology that came to dominate political debate in the 1960s was bent on removing barriers that prevented women from becoming full-fledged members of the labor force (Jonung and Thordarsson 1980:109). Unions viewed women as an alternative preferable to continued use of immigrant labor (ibid., 111). Women's policy has usually been subsumed under family and labor market concerns; in the 1960s the LO transformed its women's council into a Council for Family Affairs composed of six women and five men (Scott 1982:52). The TCO in 1970 also adopted a family policy program to facilitate work force participation by both parents, through day care, parental leagues, and nontraditional

---

*I am indebted to Diane Sainsbury for clarification of these political roles.

training and education for women. The LO's policy of "wage solidarity" (begun in the 1950s but first producing an impact on women's wages in the 1960s), aimed at closing the gap between higher- and lower-paid categories of workers, benefited women, most of whom were in lower-paid jobs, although women were not singled out as a special group for treatment (Ruggie 1986:5–6).

Yet, despite union support for women's equality in the labor force and although Swedish women constitute about 40 percent of LO membership, they are underrepresented in leadership roles (Scott 1982:54). There are only a handful of women on the National Executive Committee of the LO and few on legislative bodies and collective bargaining units of the national unions, including those with a majority of women members, although some efforts at improved representation have occurred in the last decade (Qvist, Acker, and Lorwin 1984:277). Like its American and British counterparts, the white-collar TCO seems to have a greater sensitivity to women's concerns than do blue-collar unions. In 1980, women made up 57 percent of the membership and 23 percent of the Executive Board (representation at the latter level decreased from 1980 to 1986), while at the district level, their executive representation was about 20 percent (ibid.; Scott 1982:54). (See Tables 7 and 8.) As in England, women's committees have been formed (sometimes in recognition of the inadequacy of the "family" approach that has been utilized), training courses established, and equality officers appointed, but these have been created from the top down and do not represent an independent feminist force (Qvist, Acker, and Lorwin 1984:278). Although Cook and Till Ritz (1981) suggest that there have been outspoken efforts in white-collar unions to set up women's committees, study and consciousness-raising groups, and even local-level women's caucuses, this researcher found little evidence of such activism. Equality officers lack support and resources; most do not even devote full time to their "equality" role. Among the labor unions making up the LO in 1986, only the metal workers had a full-time equality officer (interview, Carlsson, 1986). Gender-based activism seems rare in Swedish trade unions.

As a consequence and as an example of the failure to articulate a feminist perspective, there has been virtually no effort to use the Co-determination Act passed in 1977, which gives employees greater influence over the organization and content of their jobs, at the local level on behalf of women's concerns. Local unions have continued to discourage active participation by women and failed to advance women's issues through the negotiating system (Mellstrom and Sterner 1980:14). The framing of discussion about women in the guise of "equality" and "family policy" often results in failure to discuss women's issues in sexual power terms (interview, Petersson, 1986). There are in unions no autonomous women's groups that might negotiate or monitor collective agreements, nor does the union leadership seem receptive to fostering such groups.

This situation has led Hernes (1983:10) and other observers to the view that the organizations most crucial in decision-making and strategic influence—that is, those that are economically based—are even less responsive to women's power and access than electorally based ones. In such contexts, women are often powerless "policy-takers" instead of policymakers. Unlike Swedish men, Swedish women have no basis for political organization

Table 7.
Percentage of Women in Swedish Blue-Collar Trade Unions (LO) and Trade Union Offices, 1983

Union	Women Members	Congressional Delegates	National Executive	Central Negotiating Board	Regional Executives
Garment workers	68.9	52.4	28.6	23.3	49.1
Sheet metal workers	None	None	None	None	None
Building workers	1.6	0.4	None	None	0.2
Electricians	0.5	0.4	None	None	None
Factory workers	30.5	13.8	13.8	7.3	12.0
Maintenance workers	54.5	21.7	9.5	27.3	28.4
Hairdressers	93.9	87.8	94.7	71.4	83.3
Social insurance and insurance agents	71.6	37.9	30.8	20.0	39.2
Graphic industry employees	29.5	9.3	11.1	3.3	18.9
Miners	10.5	5.0	None	None	6.0
Retail and commercial employees	76.5	58.4	50.0	49.7	55.5

Hotel and restaurant workers	78.6	74.0	52.0	56.0	67.1
Municipal workers	79.2	46.2	53.8	32.3	40.8
Agricultural workers	27.7	15.0	15.8	8.7	NA*
Food employees	39.6	20.3	4.5	11.7	17.3
Metal workers	17.4	3.3	2.2	1.8	NA
Musicians	25.0	9.2	10.5	6.7	18.0
Painters	1.1	None	None	None	None
Pulp and paper workers	17.8	6.0	3.2	11.1	10.3
Seamen	12.7	9.8	30.8	7.1	NA
Forest workers	8.5	7.4	NA	4.2	1.2
State employees	27.0	10.7	12.0	9.4	15.5
Transport workers	13.1	10.2	6.2	NA	7.6
Wood industry workers	15.7	7.2	2.9	2.4	5.3
Total	41.7	21.3	18.5	20.2	20.2

SOURCE: Based on data in Landsorganisationen 1984.
* Not available.

Table 8.
*Women as Percentage of Members and Elected
Officials in Swedish Trade Union Confederations,
1977, 1980, and 1986*

	LO			TCO			SACO/SR		
	1977	1980	1986	1977	1980	1986	1977	1980	1986
Members	36	40	43	46	57	57	31	35	39
Convention delegates	18	25 (1981)	NA*	20	32	NA	24	NA	NA
General council	9	NA	14	16	NA	33	15	NA	29
Executive board	0	0	7	20	23	18	30	NA	20
National union presidents	0	0	NA	8	NA	15	8	NA	28

SOURCES: JA SAF/PTK. *Siffror om Män och Kvinnor*, Stockholm: 1987, p. 267; Qvist, Acker, and Lorwin 1984:277; and Central Statistics, *Kvinno-och Mansvarlden*, Stockholm: 1986, p. 177.
    *Not available.

in the labor sector (ibid.). The corporate channel is thus the least participative, and the most hierarchical, oligarchical, and elitist (ibid., 7).

Given the resistance to change in the still male-dominated union structures, unions are not likely to be the major route for access to power for Swedish women (Scott 1982:55). While unions support equality in the labor market, they tend to view "class differences as greater than the differences between the sexes" (Qvist, Acker, and Lorwin 1984:278). Under these circumstances, it is not difficult to see that recognition of women's interests in party structures may have only a limited parallel in unions (Scott 1982:60). Although women have gradually been increasing their role in union offices over the past two decades, in the powerful LO with strong links to the dominant Social Democratic

Party, there has been little evidence of changed attitudes toward power and policy.

Policies

Equal Opportunity

From the 1960s on, prompted by Eva Moberg's pamphlet "The Conditional Emancipation of Women," a sex-role debate was engendered and all political parties came to support equality-related policies in Sweden. As already noted, Swedish policy regarding women has been viewed as aimed at alleviating labor shortages by bringing women into the work force, with welfare and other policies directed toward this end rather than toward women's needs and concerns per se.

Eduards and her colleagues (Eduards, Halsaa, and Skjeie 1985:136) have suggested that the equality focus had a second source: economic issues so long at the core of party activity were now removed from the hands of the parties and elected representatives and placed in the administrative sector. This shift resulted in a changed relationship to societal groups and a diffusion of party divisions, giving the parties more opportunity to create a new ideological profile. Women were correctly perceived as a new source of members and voters, and the thrust toward equality policy followed accordingly. As in Britain and the United States, changing patterns of electoral politics sometimes resulted in partisan efforts to mobilize a new coalition that included women's groups.

The Swedish need for an increase in labor force participation led to a recognition of women as a large, virtually untapped labor source (Adams and Winston 1980: 187). The 1960s saw the beginning of special courses and other measures designed to induce and facilitate increased labor force participation by women as well as a debate on sex roles. First to be introduced were income tax reforms that lowered the burden on married working women by providing for separate taxation of spouses and reducing the marginal tax rate. In 1972 an Advisory Council to the Prime Minister on Equality Between Men and Women was appointed to enhance "free personal development" and alter sex roles and responsibilities (Baude 1979:151). According to Kelman (1981:28) the unusual placement of this agency in the office of the prime minister meant enhanced possibilities for close political control. In general, the council provided for experimental efforts to place women in nontraditional jobs, to shorten the workday to six hours and allow two shifts, and to provide "equality grants" for companies that train women for jobs traditionally occupied by men (Baude 1979:151). A Parliamentary Committee on Equality, appointed in 1976, continued to work on integrative policies. Thus, by the 1970s, the public discussion had turned from "sex roles" to "equality" policy.

The LO had supported efforts to reform income tax laws, day care, and parental leave (to be discussed presently). But, as in Britain, on issues of wages, hiring, and promotion the unions were reluctant to abandon their collective bargaining efforts in the interest of legislative rule-making (Qvist, Acker, and Lorwin 1984:271). Strong opposition from labor and employers was overcome only when a nonsocialist government gained power (Eduards, Halsaa, and Skjeie 1985:148). In 1976 the government enacted the first antisex discrimination act, creating an equality ombudsman and calling for affirmative action, increased representation by women on public bodies, and efforts to increase recruitment of women in male-dominated positions (Scott 1982:32). The 1976 Equality Ordinance provided for the appointment of an Equal Opportunities Commission and a full-time equality ombudsman (the first appointee was an experienced woman judge, Inga Britt Tornell) who has the right to resolve complaints.

A 1979 Act on Equality Between Men and Women prohibited sex discrimination and required employees to work actively for equality. The act's coverage is confined to groups not covered by collective agreements, which take precedence (Eduards, Halsaa, and Skjeie 1985:146). The concept of affirmative action does not really exist operationally in Sweden because there is no timetable set for compliance with the act and because the equality ombudsman cannot override collective agreements and enforce compliance (Gustaffson 1984:146). There are no statutory sanctions if employers do not comply with the legislative enactments (of the three countries examined, only in the United States have financial sanctions been employed successfully to enforce equality laws) (Jackson 1984:199). Since 1983 a national Equality Council, comprised of party representatives, women's organizations, unions, and employers, has superseded the earlier Advisory Council (Eduards, Halsaa, and Skjeie 1985:139).

In 1977, the LO and the TCO signed equality agreements with the Swedish Employers Confederation (SAF) covering all workers in the private work force. The agreement banned all discrimination and called for equality-related measures. Cases to be settled were to go to the tripartite Labour Court. In the three years between the signing of equality agreements and 1980 when an amended version went into effect, no cases went to the Labour Court under the LO-SAF agreement. It is doubtful that the absence of complaints signifies the absence of problems; rather, the concern about producing conflict, the lack of a feminist presence, and the unfamiliarity of this approach may limit its effectiveness (Qvist, Acker, and Lorwin 1984:272).

In a society where a tradition of special women's groups has not existed since 1900 (only local women's clubs that haven't much influence endure) (interview, Carlsson, 1986), unions appear to be reluctant to act once a complaint has been made. They are especially remiss in taking action on job recruitment, let alone wages and salaries. Originally opposed to the idea of legislation to deal with sex equality, they have never been very enthusiastic about aiding the process of compliance (interview, Wadstein, 1986).

The "equality grants" have not proven successful. Since 1980, only 693 trainees have been placed in jobs, just 1.5 percent of all trainees (Qvist, Acker, and Lorwin 1984:271–72). Given the small incentive, or subsidy, of 20 SEK (Swedish kronor—at the current U.S. exchange rate of about 70 cents to the krona) for each trainee and the narrow range of possible occupations covered, the lack of compliance is not surprising. Another measure, part of Sweden's regional policy, which mandated gender-based quotas (40 percent women) in new firms or industries in Sweden's outlying areas, met with mixed results during 1974–79.

Numerous unions have set up equality committees, special training forces, and other groups directed particularly at women. Nonetheless, the results of private-sector efforts seem disappointing: in four years of subsidies to firms to hire women for male-dominated occupations, only about 1,000, or one-tenth of 1 percent, of the female labor force were hired (ibid., 270–71).

Under the Social Democratic government that returned to power in 1982, a Ministry for Equality and Immigration was established in the Department of Labour. Among the directives given to this new agency: change the conditions for women, change the roles of men, influence policy, and aid immigrant women (interview, Lidbeck 1986). The ministry has thus far sought to spend its rather substantial budget (15 million SEK) to promote courses for young girls to broaden their choices in order to break the pronounced pattern of occupational segregation in all areas of life. There has been little evaluation research done to assess "success," because "they are not sure how to go about it" (ibid.). As for the mandate to change men's attitudes, thus far no conclusions have been reached on how to implement it.

The equality ombudsman, Inga Britt Tornell, has received enthusiastic support from many Swedish women for her forthright activism. However, with a staff of only seven, the tasks for the ombudsman appear formidable. The tasks are 1) taking complaints to the Labour Court, 2) supervising employers, and 3) molding public opinion (interview, Wadstein, 1986). The ombudsman's office has been particularly effective with regard to the last task: four times a year it issues a report, *Jamsides,* and it has released over 20,000 copies of an excellent statistical and factual compendium on women in Sweden entitled *Side by Side* (Equality Ministry 1985). The ombudsman has even tackled the issue of women priests in the Swedish Church, albeit unsuccessfully. The ombudsman may issue injunctions only on employment discrimination initiated by individuals, employee organizations, or by the ombudsman office itself. The office responds to about 150 complaints per year. Numerous observers, including the deputy ombudsman, point to the difficulty of getting women to make complaints in a culture that does not value aggressive individualists. Issues of equal pay for work of equal value have thus far not moved beyond the discussion stage. The commission's work is somewhat constrained by the fact that it does not have the right to request documentation in discrimination cases in the private sector.

Only several hundred cases have come before the ombudsman, and just nine cases were taken by her to the Labour Court through 1984. The four settled at that time resulted in financial compensation, but no requirement was made for remedial action by the employer with regard to either the individual involved or the discriminatory practice (Ruggie 1984:178; Qvist, Acker, and Lorwin 1984:273). Several observers have concluded that the law establishing the ombudsman's office has few teeth and is not very effective. As Karin Andersson, the former chair of the Swedish Equality Committee, commented, "It is difficult to struggle for something on which, formally, everyone agrees" (quoted in Eduards, Halsaa, and Skjeie 1985:141). In this context, Swedish equality agencies may be seen more as channeling pressure regarding discrimination than responding to it.

Social Policies

No account of public policy regarding women in Sweden would be complete without a discussion of related social policies. In 1976 an abortion act was passed that gives women the right to abortion on request up to the eighteenth week of pregnancy, largely a ratification of practices already common. (After the twelfth week a special investigation is held to judge the risks; after the eighteenth week the abortion may be granted only by the Board of Health.) This policy was not widely perceived as a women's issue; rather, debate centered on the social and economic costs of unwanted children.

As early as 1945, Swedish women were entitled to six months' maternity leave—without pay. In 1974 the well-known parental insurance law was passed that gave fathers as well as mothers the right to paid leave of absence following birth of a child. The benefit was roughly equivalent to 90 percent of lost income for seven months (Baude 1979:158). In 1978, the period for parental leave was extended to nine months. In practice, women still use the parental leave provisions most frequently. In 1976 the number of fathers exercising their right to stay home was 10 percent; the number has never been higher than 12 percent (ibid., 170; Qvist, Acker, and Lorwin 1984:270). Men may also take 15 days of leave at the time of a child's birth. Either parent may also take paid sick leave of up to 60 days a year to care for a sick child. Men who take such leave do so only for a few days, whereas women are more likely to extend their periods of absence (Jonung and Thordarsson 1980:133).

Day care, long a concern of the LO in the interest of increasing female labor force participation, was endorsed by the Riksdag in the 1970s. Efforts to increase, by 1980, the number of places available for children during and after school care were intended to further the goal of providing publicly supported day care for the children of all parents who work through a system of state subsidies (Baude 1979:161). The actual increase fell short of the goal. A new goal of 100 percent of day-care places has been set for 1991. No plan for implementing this new stage of expansion to meet demand has yet been presented. At the time of this writing, the number of day-care places still lags far behind the necessary numbers, especially considering the high number of women in the labor force; about 60 percent of the children from one to five are housed in community-supported family day-care homes or public day-care centers ("Child Care Programs in Sweden" 1984). Nonetheless, available day-care places have risen rapidly since 1966, when the policy was initiated, and programs are well staffed and regulated, in contrast to their British and American counterparts.

The Swedish tradition of public education is unlike that of most of Western Europe and of the United States in that children do not begin school until the age of seven, and even at that time school hours are limited. This situation exacerbates the problem of finding day-care places for a larger population. Children from ages seven to 12 who require after-school care are usually unable to obtain it (only 17 percent were in public facilities in the mid-1980s). Because the extent of day care in a given community depends largely on local initiatives, the variance between rural and urban availability may be great.

Since 1979, parents of children under eight may work a six-hour day, at a reduced salary; they may remain at home full-time with a child up to one and a half years old. Child minders are available for sick children (although they may exist more in principle than in reality, as one professional woman remarked that they are often available only after the children are well) and even on weekends, a particularly thoughtful aspect of the Swedish social policy for single parents. Single-parent families are given higher maintenance subsidies than two-parent families; unlike the situation in the United States, there are few social or economic stigmas attached to divorce or out-of-wedlock births (Boneparth 1984:135).

The state makes direct payments to all families with children in the form of generous child allowances, housing subsidies, and advance payments on maintenance allowances (Wistrand 1982:21). This last form of aid means that in effect the state has taken over the burden of child support from absent fathers and shores up single-parent families.

Other Women-related Policies

Two other issues related to public policy and women also relate to sexual politics: rape and domestic violence.

Rape has not been publicly perceived as a major problem in Sweden, a nation in which crimes of violence seem rare. This attitude has been one explanation for the absence of a rape crisis movement in Sweden. Nonetheless, the incidence of rape annually is about 10,000 reported cases, the number having risen steeply with a greater willingness to file charges (Equality Ministry 1985:74). In 1976 the women's organizations of all the major parties as well as numerous other women's groups protested a proposed change in the rape law that would have permitted the courts to take into account the previous sexual behavior of the victim. The outcry and pressure of this all-party women's effort were sufficiently strong to lead to the creation of a new commission to rewrite the law. As of 1984, a new law was passed entitling women suffering assault to have someone with them during legal proceedings. The prior sexual behavior of the victim is not to be taken into account, nor is the victim's relationship to the offender. Legal aid for victims is now possible in some cases and is likely to be expanded in the future (ibid.).

The issue of domestic violence attracted belated (in

comparison with the issue in the United States and Britain) but intense interest in Sweden primarily in the 1980s. In 1978, the first Woman's House under the auspices of a feminist group in Göteborg (Gothenburg), combining a shelter with other activities, was opened. Elsewhere, as in Orebro, the community was responsible for funding a crisis center. It appears that more avowedly feminist groups have sometimes had difficulty obtaining funding from their local councils; nonetheless, about a hundred shelters exist today in Sweden (interview, Hedlund, 1986). Because Sweden lacks both a philanthropic and a voluntary action tradition and citizens expect the state to assume responsibility for all social services and needs, the likelihood of an independent shelter movement enduring is limited. Funding is sometimes forthcoming at the municipal level, and the National Organization for Women's Shelters (RUKS) has been established. This new organization is entitled to special funding of about 100,000 SEK annually from a special government fund created for women's groups (interview, Ohnfelt, 1986). Wife beating has been open to public prosecution only since 1982. At that time the law was amended so that the victimized woman herself did not have to prefer charges against the man or plead in court. Domestic assault had formerly been indictable only by information, meaning that no charges could be filed unless the woman herself reported them. The change means that a neighbor or police officer can prefer charges, the upshot being an increase in the number of complaints filed (Equality Ministry 1985:73).

Although the shelter movement initially was feminist in impetus, and marks a rare case of public acceptance, as in the United States today its influences are mixed (interview, Boye, 1986). Shelter employees are paid and view their work as a job just like any other. National action on battered women has been followed by a report undertaken by the Social Services Department of the government. However, statistics on the actual incidence of domestic violence are exceedingly difficult to obtain. The treatment of offending males seems to have taken a somewhat different turn in Sweden than in the United Kingdom and, especially, the United States. In the main, punishment, other than short jail sentences, is often eschewed in favor of providing therapeutic treatment for men. A men's shelter has even been formed in Göteborg to provide support for troubled men. Hence, the Swedish approach stresses rehabilitation rather than punitive treatment, with offenders also seen as "victims" (Equality Ministry 1985:75). As of March 1985, the Swedish government decided to award grants to encourage shelters to develop their activities further.

Assessment

In Sweden, women's organizations have little impact either on public authorities or on public policy per se (Hernes and Hanninen-Salmelin 1985:108). Gender is not seen as an explicitly deliberate or legitimate dimension of politics in Scandinavia (Hernes 1984:39) despite the presence of a large number of women in legislative politics.

Swedish women (the "daughters of the welfare state") (Eduards 1986:15) appear to have many of the demands of their feminist sisters elsewhere taken care of by the state and political system, yet their concerns seem to be almost obscured by the efforts to reach equality that are, in the main, not the result of their own efforts. In 1973, Rita Liljestrom (quoted in Scott 1982:157) wrote that if women are to achieve collective liberation, they "need to rally around a community of values, around a program which roots them in shared experiences, and which gives them political identity for 'sisterhood' and an alternative value system to keep them from being devoured by equality under the terms set by the male value system." This course has not been followed in Sweden, nor has there been a public dialogue on women's issues conducted by women on *their* terms. As Baude (1979), among others, points out, women's liberation and feminism have been viewed as confrontational and "anti-Swedish."

There is limited room for experimentation and grassroots efforts in a society in which all is encompassed by the state. Hence, issues like rape, wife battering, and other aspects of male power, violence, and domination have only begun to be raised in this society so devoted to the establishment of equality in a sex-neutral fashion. Nonetheless, even when grass-roots level efforts are made—for example, to develop female-operated refuges for battered women—they are soon incorporated by the state. As Cheri Register (quoted in Eduards, Halsaa, and Skjeie 1985 : 159) puts it,

> When conflicts have arisen in Sweden and demands are put forth by different groups, they must be swallowed quickly by the all-encompassing Social Democracy. Social Democracy must show without delay that it is also capable of coping with the new demands emanating from women. In other words, the special interests of women have been subordinated to the general good, the definition of which still lies in the hands of men. . . . Reforms can also be considered as a preventive measure—one which is necessary to divert more radical demands and conflicts which could lead to a more serious split.

In this type of system, significant issues regarding male-female relations and power are rarely seriously discussed as topics of public debate. Autonomous women's organizations are viewed as suspect, and women are deterred from shaping policy on their own terms. While today some activity around single-issue feminist concerns exists, there is little evidence of the past dynamic efforts made by women, especially in political parties in the 1960s and 1970s.

There can be no doubt that Sweden's social support system, especially for single-female heads of families and for all women in the labor force, is superior and perhaps without equal in the Western world. (The one exception is day care, which is still inadequate and lags far behind the near-universal *écoles maternelles* system provided by the French government, which seeks to respond to the educational and personal needs of each child.) Nevertheless, it should be recalled that welfare, however progressive, is not synonymous with power and the ability to shape one's own status (Hernes 1984: 32–33). "Qualitative" gender issues, unrelated to economic concerns, have been neglected in a system that defines equality almost exclusively in economic terms (Kesselman and Krieger 1987:528).

Because the rhetoric of equality has been widely accepted in Sweden, it is difficult to move beyond it to new approaches. Women are objects of state welfare policies that they have had only a limited role in shaping. There is need for greater scope for the articulation of women's interests, which may result in a more truly egalitarian society. (Eduards [1986:15] makes a similar point.) However, it is especially difficult to organize effectively in a society in which everything has been organized and in which the expectation that society will care for all needs animates most social endeavor (interview, Dahlberg, 1986). Against this backdrop, efforts by women at the grass roots to stress some feminist concerns have been noteworthy, though often short-lived. The emphasis on the need for organization is, of course, particularly incongruent with feminist notions of participation and structure, making the route of radical feminism especially problematic in Sweden.

Sweden's most unique contribution is the effort to change women's status by addressing inequality for men and women alike. An equal-opportunities mentality pervades society and policy-making; the emphasis on sex neutrality coupled with cooperation has produced a system in which women's issues are no longer perceived as a problem and are almost wholly integrated into family and social policy (Hernes 1982:7). Nonetheless, thus far equality has been defined exclusively in male terms. As most Swedish women interviewed for this study agreed, gender-neutral policies in a society still highly stratified by gender end up by benefiting the already powerful—that is, males. That Swedish women have far outnumbered men in the degree to which they wish to use ad hoc political activity (39 to 6 percent, respectively) suggests how poorly they feel themselves to be integrated into the political structure. This is one area of Swedish politics in which women constitute a plurality (Peterson 1984:12)!

We are left with the view that "society does not change just because laws do" (Gold 1977:11), that rule-making may be insufficient in the absence of grass-roots organizations to aid in carrying out the rules. Even policy on sex neutrality has been framed in the guise of recommendations, not dictates, making compliance exceedingly difficult (Eduards 1986:15).

Although Swedish policies are held up as models for women in other nations, they have also demonstrated the intransigence of problems of sexual inequality and the possible limits of a system structured so totally around consensus. The labor market remains highly segregated, with women concentrated in low-paying, low-status jobs to an ever greater degree than in other nations (UNESCO 1983:30). Income differentials, though narrowed, remain significant, and close to 50 percent of Swedish women are primarily part-time workers in the labor force. The acceptance of part-time work by most women locks them into traditional family roles and creates few opportunities for pursuit of serious careers, especially in terms of training and promotion. The problem appears to lie in the failure to address the sexual division of labor in the home and in the workplace, partially because women's issues have rarely been raised as a concern apart from economic and labor market considerations. The division of labor reflected in the home, in a society still wed to many traditional values regarding sexual roles, is reflected in the larger political and economic society as well, as the marginal position of women in these sectors suggests. Sex segregation continues to exist not only in the labor force but also in the political roles to which women are limited, thus preventing them from advancing into meaningful careers. The anti-individualist rhetoric of Swedish socialism has in this instance kept women in their place.

The Swedish experience suggests that even benevolent state efforts to integrate women into existing political and economic structures may be insufficient in the attainment of role transformation if they are not accompanied by other changes as well. It has been the contention of this chapter that, coupled with the widespread acceptance of the ideology of gender equality, if not its practice, the absence of independent women's organizations that generate debate regarding sex roles and power in society may be crucial. Despite the real success of many of the highly institutionalized Swedish efforts to eradicate gender inequality, the system appears to have reached an impasse.

6

Conclusion

This study has examined the different directions taken by feminism in three nations, emphasizing the importance of external factors, including political institutions, cultural traits, and values on the resulting movement structures and goals.

Swedish politics, we have found, presents a model of consensus and corporatism, as well as an all-encompassing state that directs most citizen-related activity and tends to incorporate those activities existing outside the boundaries of state policy. The British system is distinguished by a centralized bureaucratic state and a "dichotomous" ideological context in which conflictual politics tend to predominate. In the United States a less organized, somewhat adversarial pluralism reigns in a system distrustful of centralized power and welfare policies. In turn, the character of feminism has been shaped by the character of the state as well as economic factors and the strength (or weakness) of traditional values and attitudes. Thus, we have argued that in Sweden a form of state equality concerning women exists in the absence of an organized movement (albeit with a feminist "presence," primarily in the sphere of elective partisan politics). In Britain, ideological/left-wing feminism is in part a product of the closed and conflictual political system. In the United States, a less ideological and more pragmatic political setting has led to a mass-based liberal/equal rights feminism. The prevalent mode of activism has been interest group lobbying for power rather than integration in parties and unions in the manner of the European movements.

In this concluding chapter, we assess the societal impact and success of each approach to equality and self-determination for women.

Definitions of what constitutes social movement "success" may vary. Success may refer to legitimization of a group's goals, change in individual or group consciousness, and/or change in public policy outcomes involving redistribution of social goals and changes in power relations (Jenkins 1983:544). For some, political access for hitherto excluded groups constitutes success. Success may also refer to the mere fact of survival, and/or the creation of alternative sources of power through the development of new organizational forms (Rowbotham 1983:136). It is evident that the movement in each nation has succeeded in different terms, partially because of different goals and the systemic factors that constrain political activism.

We have shown that the most active part of the British feminist movement emphasizes expressiveness, personal transformation, consciousness, and changed belief systems. It eschews formal structure and hierarchy and is centered in small groups that stress life experience and self-help politics. In Gerlach and Hine's (1970:

55) terms, it is segmented—localized, autonomous, and ever changing—and decentralized. Nonetheless, it lacks the *reticulate,* or networking structure that they see as inherent to movement groupings. Largely as a result of ideological conflicts and the consequent failure to coordinate action and permit the sharing of resources, networking efforts, particularly important at the national level, are absent. Social movement organizations in the United States have been far more likely to form coalitions in order to realize their goals (McCarthy and Zald 1977).

As several researchers (Zald and Ash 1966; Curtis and Zurcher 1974) point out, movements adopt different forms depending on their goals, with personal change movements adapting decentralized structures and exclusive membership, while institutional change movements are typically centralized and inclusive. Although the goals of grass-roots participation, service, and transformation of aims are more likely to be realized in decentralized structures, the costs may lie in the failure to influence the larger political system, as in the British case. Bureaucratic structures provide skill and coordination but may sacrifice participatory goals, as is sometimes true of the American movement (Zald and Ash 1966). One trend in the United Kingdom that may effectively interact with the structure and values that predominate among women's groups is the growing interest of local council governments in aiding feminist efforts.

Clearly, the British movement has succeeded in creating local activities emphasizing consciousness and lifestyle transformation in numerous (primarily urban) centers throughout the country. British feminism has also defied traditional sociological rules regarding the origins and maintenance of social movements. Rather than becoming bureaucratized and less radical, the British movement has retained its ideological fervor and commitment and has continued to seek new alternative structures (Bouchier 1984:179). The degree of activism and commitment is impressive, even to the casual observer. Movement groupings and activist outposts created in the 1970s survive. These include Women in the Media, NAC, the NWAF, Rights of Women (the voluntary legal arm of British feminism), and the Women's Rights unit of the NCCL, as well as Women Against Violence Against Women (WAVAW) (Van der Gaag 1985: 137). As Jenson (1982:373) has observed, the movement's main contribution may be simply its survival, in contrast to the largely esoteric state of the formerly active French and Italian (as well as other continental) movements. The British movement remains the most vital and important one in Europe, although the numbers involved in some grass-roots groups may have declined since the 1970s (Coultas 1981:36).

Although the British movement's origins were in many ways similar to those in the United States (even prompted initially by infusions of Americans who served as catalysts), the movement was never characterized by either mass demonstrations (other than the Corrie effort discussed earlier) or a strong national presence. Its internecine struggles, largely between sectors of radical and socialist feminism, remain unresolved. One effort in conjunction with the TUC—the march to fight restrictions in the abortion act, demonstrated both the mass potential of the movement and its internal conflicts. This march was probably the largest demonstration over a social issue that Britain had ever seen (Bassnett 1986:157). Nonetheless, it revealed the chasm between women and the trade union movement and between so-

cialist and radical feminists. The radical feminists re-
sented what they perceived as male usurpation of the
movement (as women were placed fifth in a seven-place
march) and ran to the front with their banners. Three
women were arrested in a later scuffle with police for
hoisting the women's liberation banner; a feeling of
hostility was thus one result of the day's effort, though
not the only one. The effort at the Greenham Common
missile installation three years later resolved some of
these conflicts through a separatist, women-only protest. Thirty thousand strong, it helped to bring women
from all groups together and to generate widespread
awareness of the dangers of nuclear proliferation. A
major question for British feminism remains the cen-
trality of "cultural" versus "political" feminism, a question we will return to because of its significance in
the movement's failure to create a meaningful national
presence.

In the United Kingdom, parties and unions occupy a
major—if declining—political role, and a tradition of
left/socialist thought has been strong. Although activity
in party and trade union politics may be viewed as
equivalent to the American liberal/equal rights movement, little evidence for this perspective exists. This
analysis is thus in considerable disagreement with the
view expressed by Hewlett (1986:170), who argues that
in both England and Sweden the most effective women's
groups have been embedded in parties and unions, not
in separate feminist organizations. Rather, it appears
that women's participation in established British institutions has been marked by marginalization, with
women organized into separate advisory groups and
limited to a handful of mandated seats on executive
committees. The major union force, the TUC, has en-

dorsed, lobbied for, and even demonstrated for numerous progressive policies on behalf of women (especially in the case of abortion, referred to earlier). Nonetheless, where issues of economic and political power are involved, there is greater hesitancy.

In addition, tensions exist between socialism and feminism and between the hierarchical unions/parties and feminist ideology, as the march against the Corrie Bill demonstrated. However, at their most effective, women's groups within parties may serve as forums through which women's demands and concerns can be highlighted. Nonetheless, Jenson's (1982:370) contention that British feminism has emerged from a decade of political isolation and an exclusive grass-roots focus to help unite the Left and the Labour Party seems premature, based on the analysis presented here. The energetic activity of women within Labour and the organized Left notwithstanding, thus far their policy- and decision-making impact has been limited.

Despite the existence of numerous progressive policies pertaining to women in the United Kingdom, the absence of a feminist movement that can set a policy agenda, speak for itself, and engage in dialogue regarding specific policy initiatives has resulted in serious gaps between policy and implementation. The upshot: a strangely limited vision of feminist goals and ideals, which has, in fact, led to less societal change than might be expected.

In the United States a tradition of reform, the absence of a strong socialist Left, and the impact of interest groups in decision-making have combined to produce a different type of movement. In part reflecting the increased weakness of parties and unions politically, feminists have organized as separatist or gender-based groups outside established structures (Adams and Winston 1980:104). This approach has given them significant autonomy in strategy, as a recent trend in the direction of electoral efforts demonstrates. American feminism is characterized by far greater inclusivity of different views than its British counterpart; coalition building and networking are movement watchwords. The American movement has also forged an accommodation between the more "radical" women's liberation movement and the middle-class reformist one (it has also developed strong linkages with traditional women's groups, such as the League of Women Voters and the YWCA).

The most visible manifestation of American feminism is the traditional interest group, organized as a hierarchical structure with staff dominance. Groups such as NOW have moved in the direction of mass membership, while such feminist groups as WEAL, the Center for Women Policy Studies, and the NWPC fit the McCarthy/Zald model of funded social movement organizations relying on "conscience constituencies" or contributors for resources and staff for day-to-day decision-making and long-term strategizing (Handler 1978:8; McCarthy and Zald 1975:11). As the history of the movement against domestic violence demonstrates, even nontraditional groups with grass-roots origins are pulled toward political engagement and greater professionalization. American feminists have been eclectic and pragmatic in their use of strategies—from protest to litigation and campaigning. Nonetheless, although American feminist groups have moved much further than British ones in the direction of traditional organizational structure (which most reformist lobbying groups have always utilized in the United States), they have not abandoned feminist policy goals in the interests of organizational maintenance. Thus, although different from their British counterparts in structure and ideology, the movements have each remained firmly committed to their own feminist vision of the "good society."

In Sweden, feminist movement politics per se has played a minor role, although "equality" and "family" issues have been given primacy by the SDP and other parties. Women's federations in four of Sweden's five parties have provided a context for some policies pertaining to women and for recruitment of women to party and political office. Although various data in this chapter suggest that women are dissatisfied with Swedish efforts to achieve "equality," at present apparently no mechanism exists to capitalize on this discontent and move beyond the egalitarian rhetoric (so dominant a feature in Swedish society) to a new stage of political endeavor on behalf of women.

So far in this chapter, we have examined the role of women's politics in changing individual consciousness, creating alternative political structures, and simply surviving as organizational structures. Hence, we have been concerned with movements (or their absence) primarily at the individual and structural/organizational level. Now, recalling our initial definitions of movement success, we will examine other facets of the success, or impact, of women's politics: 1) the impact on changed policy outcomes and 2) the impact on group and societal consciousness as well as the legitimization of group goals (see Table 9). To assess the latter, in particular, we rely on attitudinal and economic data on the three nations under consideration. We will try to distinguish between those gains that have been made in the welfare state and those that have involved a changed role for

Table 9.
Impact of Changes in Individual and Group Consciousness

	Sweden	U.K.	U.S.
Legitimation of group goals	−	−	+
Access to power structure	+	−	+
Changes in power relations	+	−	+
Public policy outcomes	+ +	+	+ +
Group survival	−	+	+ +
Creation of alternative sources of power	−	+	+ +

NOTE: − = little or none; + = somewhat; + + = significant.

women in society because of increased economic opportunities. We will divide our discussion into 1) attitudes that demonstrate consciousness of the women's movement and support for feminist issues, 2) attitudes toward child care and domestic work—or the persistence of traditional attitudes toward sex roles, and 3) evidence of changed economic roles for women as a result of more employment opportunities.

Extent of Support for Feminist Movements

We have already noted that the British movement has succeeded in changing the consciousness of its individual members and in creating new, localized alternative power and service structures. With regard to other measures of success—for instance, those involving the larger society and policy outcomes—the movement's achievements have been less impressive. Efforts to increase collective awareness of movement goals and to gain broadened support within the political system may involve potential members, allies, and the general public. Measured by this standard, the total membership of British feminist activists has been estimated as one-tenth of 1 percent (or 20,000) of the female population, indicating a huge distance to go to reach even a fraction of the women in the United Kingdom (Bouchier 1984:178). In contrast, membership in traditional British women's groups is close to a million (ibid.). Only a small segment of British women have been reached by the women's liberation movement in its various manifestations, and the movement remains isolated, both by deliberate design and because of the obstacles created by British economic and political institutions. Despite the mobilization potential evident in the case of abortion rights and Greenham Common, the movement remains on the fringes of British life, its marginal position reinforced by media emphasis on the movement's domination by antimale radical feminists. The failure to reach more traditional women may be seen in a 1981 *Spare Rib* poll that compared the responses of *Spare Rib* readers (associated with the women's liberation movement) with women in the more traditional Townswomen's Guilds (see Table 10).

Similarly, despite the media attention given the women's protest at Greenham Common in December 1982, there is little evidence that most women have changed their opinion about the cruise missile as a result of that effort. The balance of women had the same opinion after the demonstrations as they had had three years earlier (*Spare Rib*, May 1984:18). A *Guardian* poll in January 1983 showed about 23 percent of women to be in favor of the Greenham Common activists' goal— that Britain abandon nuclear weapons—which was actually 10 percent fewer than four months earlier (before the protest). *Spare Rib* rightfully concludes that Greenham has not especially raised women's awareness of the

Table 10.
Attitudes of Spare Rib *Readers and Members of Townswomen's Guilds Toward Work by Women*

	SR	TG
Bad for children	7%	75%
Undermines the family	16%	71%

SOURCE: *Spare Rib*, November 1981:24.

nuclear threat, at least as measured by national polls. In conducting their own, more limited poll, most women interviewed by *Spare Rib* objected to the all-female nature of the protest, and the magazine's survey found that working-class women were less supportive of the Greenham Common protest and of feminism than their middle-class sisters (ibid., 19–20).

The American movement has grown in size and heterogeneity, particularly in the Reagan era, where apparent disaster has been turned to advantage in terms of group mobilization. NOW, for example, grew from 125,000 (in 1978) to 250,000 in several years. This number has fluctuated considerably as the attention of the public has wandered from one issue to another (similar phenomena have been observed with regard to other reform groups) (McFarland 1984:203; Bomafede 1986: 2175). As of 1985, the dues-paying membership of the feminist movement numbered about 300,000 (Gelb and Palley 1987:26). Despite the relatively small membership (augmented considerably if the million-odd members of the more traditional women's groups allied with feminists are added), support for feminists among the American populace appears to be far broader and more significant than is the case in Britain.

American women's support for feminism also appears

to be substantial: 56 percent of them said in 1986 they considered themselves feminist, 28 percent said they were not, and a mere 4 percent indicated they were anti-feminists (*Newsweek*, March 31, 1986:51). A majority of women also indicated that the women's movement had affected their lives positively (18 percent very much, 53 percent fairly much). A 1981 poll indicated that 4 percent of women and 2 percent of men contributed to the women's rights movement (about 4.5 million people), and that one of every 300 women is active in some type of feminist activity (Bouchier 1984:180). A survey by Janet Boles (1984:84) as far back as 1974 found that the total membership of women's rights groups (including the NWPC, NOW, the League of Women Voters, and the National Federation of Business and Professional Women's Clubs) was 56.77 per 10,000, indicating a fairly significant pattern of participation, which is likely to be much higher a decade later, given the trends we have outlined. As Ruth Mandel (quoted in Bomafede 1986: 2175) has noted, "The women's rights movement is in a process of diffusion. It is spread, assimilated and incorporated throughout society at various levels and [has] become part of the social fabric." Underscoring acceptance of many feminist views were the results of a recent *New York Times* poll. Twenty-eight percent of those surveyed indicated that the women's movement had made their lives better, and these respondents were most likely to be young and educated. Among those who responded favorably, improved job opportunities were cited most often as being a result of the women's movement (*New York Times*, Dec. 19, 1983:316). Similarly, while strong differences separate college-educated women from their more traditional (and more numerous) sisters, over the past decade the more egalitarian views of the former have begun to make inroads among the latter (Poole and Zeigler 1985: vii), and we contend that American sex role attitudes have become increasingly egalitarian. Growing numbers of less-educated women were found in a recent study to be more receptive to egalitarian views, although not necessarily to what is perceived as the more "radical" women's liberation movement (ibid., 10–24).

In the United States a 1980 survey found that, on a five-point scale, attitudes changed from 3.2 to 2.9 toward liberation, while in Britain rightward shifts on women's rights, abortion, and welfare were more evident (Robertson 1984:236). In Sweden, as we noted earlier, women's liberation is viewed as anathema by many men, hostility to the movement apparently existing out of all proportion to the limited strength of feminist organizations and views, at least among elite males. In any event, Swedish surveys do not reveal women's attitudes regarding feminism, because the movement in Sweden has been oriented differently. In the United Kingdom there appears to be considerable ambivalence regarding the movement, its accomplishments, and the potential role of women (despite the political success of a female prime minister), although British women are only a bit less opposed to traditional role constraints than are their American counterparts (Dex and Shaw 1986:25). While four-fifths of Americans say they would vote for a qualified woman for president (up from one-third in 1937) (Bianchi and Spahn 1986:238), in Britain, after Thatcher's election as prime minister, 64 percent agreed that it made no difference whether a woman held the office, while 25 percent said a woman was "not as good." Support for the notion of "greater confidence" in a woman as a member of Parliament has dropped

Table 11.
*Favorable Feeling Toward
Women's Liberation Movement*

Country	Parents	Offspring
United Kingdom	43%	38.1%
United States	45.7%	51.8%

SOURCE: Allerbuck, Jennings, and Rosenmayr 1979:497.

(from 5 percent of men and 12 percent of women supportive in 1975 to 2 percent and 4 percent, respectively, in 1983), perhaps reflecting some defection of women from Thatcher's social policies (*International Gallup Poll* 1981:177, 273).

Studies comparing attitudes toward feminism and women's social role in the United States and Britain also offer some striking differences. One study found British youth much less supportive of women's liberation than their European or American counterparts, suggesting that generational change has been far more limited in the United Kingdom (see Table 11).

Of particular note is the limited nature of value change that has taken place in the United Kingdom. Inglehart (1977:34) found that Britain exhibited the smallest amount of generational change of any nation in his cross-country survey. Another report of intra-European opinion on feminism reveals British women (and men) to hold a higher proportion of negative views than citizens of any other European nation except Italy. The degree of polarization cutting male/female lines is notable (Hernes 1983: Table 6). Although strictly comparable data are difficult to obtain, a 1979 poll showed 63 percent of Americans and only 40 percent of the British agreeing that the part played by women in their nation had changed a lot (*International Gallup Poll* 1981: 272). Britons are reported to have the poorest opinion of women's liberation of any Europeans (*Euro-Barometer* 1983:179).

Attitudes Toward Sex Roles

A 1983 survey found more Britons "disagreeing with women who claim there should be fewer differences between men's and women's role in society" than in any other European nation surveyed, as well as profounder disagreements regarding female family roles (e.g., housework and child care) than elsewhere in Europe (ibid., 134, 137). More British men preferred that their wives not be in paid employment (ibid., 164). These findings are confirmed by a recent survey that found that British husbands were not supportive of working wives: only 41 percent of women said their husbands were enthusiastic about their working. While in many instances working wives were tolerated by their husbands, this was true only if their employment did not interfere with their domestic life or the husband's work (*Employment Gazette*, May 1984:206).

Female attitudes toward work have undergone considerable transformation, with only 25 percent of women indicating that women's place should remain in the home; a majority believe that work is beneficial for women (ibid., 203). Among younger women, a vast majority say they wish to return to work after having children. However, 53 percent of British women (in contrast to 21 percent of American and 35 percent of Swedish women) say that women should quit their jobs when they have children and return to work only after their children are grown up (Hastings and Hastings 1985: 714). At the same time, British women accept the view that work is beneficial, but only if it can balance with and accommodate their primary domestic role (*Employment Gazette,* May 1984:203). Opposition to feminism may combine with the poor economic conditions in Britain to reinforce the concept of the "family wage" discussed earlier and keep women in a secondary role in the labor force.

British women consider their career less important than their home. Eighty-nine percent of surveyed women of working age felt that a woman's first duty was to home responsibilities, 61 percent said that a woman's first duty was to her marriage, and only 31 percent thought they could be loyal both to marriage and to a job. For 69 percent, their husband's career had priority—and 55 percent of the respondents were under 25 (Rose 1986:159)! While a poll of Townswomen's Guild respondents did reveal that a majority (69 percent) supported the view that it was good for women to work, 75 percent indicated that such work was "bad for children" and 71 percent thought that it was undermining the family (*Spare Rib,* Nov. 1981:24). Forty-eight percent of men and 38 percent of women interviewed in 1979 agreed that women should remain at home with children under 10 (*International Gallup Poll* 1981:272).

In contrast, in the United States, 63 percent of women interviewed in one poll indicated that they would want to work outside the home in the future, even if they had enough money to live comfortably without working. Another poll found a majority of American women indicating they wished to combine home and career, while slightly under half of men and women interviewed said they favored a new concept of marriage in which husband and wife share work and domestic responsibilities (*Ms.*, July 1984:60; Roper Organization 1980:30–33). By 1982, 75 percent of Americans said they approved of women working outside the home, and over 80 percent favored joint responsibility for raising children (Bianchi and Spahn 1986:239). In 1985, only 22 percent (down from 57 percent in 1967) of American college freshmen interviewed said they believe the activities of married women are best confined to the home (*Chronicle of Higher Education*, Nov. 5, 1986:32). Even women's Political Action Committees are increasingly approved by the American public—with favorable responses rising from 11 percent in November 1982 to 64 percent in May 1984 (Hastings and Hastings 1985:374). (In 1985, support for union PACs was recorded as 34 percent.)

In Britain, compulsory military service for women is favored by 35 percent of the public; in the United States, by 53 percent (Hastings and Hastings 1982:262–63). In all three of the societies under study, women continue to perform more household tasks than men, but in the United States, particularly, there is some evidence of more equal sharing of tasks, especially child care and economic roles (e.g., bill paying) (Bianchi and Spahn 1986:231).

Data collected by the University of Wisconsin's Comparative Project on Class Structure and Class Consciousness* indicate similar attitudes by U.S. and Swedish respondents toward sex roles, with one exception. As the data in Table 12 show, the exception is that whereas 66 percent of American women believe that traditional learned sex roles benefit the family, almost 60% of Swed-

---

*Data were made available by Bonnie Amim, Institute for Research on Poverty, University of Wisconsin.

Table 12.
Attitudes Toward Sex Roles
(Percentage of Respondents Agreeing)

	U.S.	Sweden
Traditional roles benefit family	66%	41%
Housework should be shared equally	95%	97%
Not enough women are employed in business	77%	85%

ish women disagree. Egalitarian attitudes toward housework are similar in both countries. Perhaps reflecting
the economic stratification in Sweden that we will discuss later, even more Swedish than American women
would like to see a larger role for their sex in business.

Other Swedish data reveal some division between
parties on ideological lines—and, increasingly, divisions between men and women—on women's issues.
The data over time suggest a trend toward conservatism
regarding some issues, a trend that may affect women
adversely in the welfare state. Growing imbalances in
the economy appear to make cuts in public expenditures
inevitable (Erickson and Aberg 1987:13). Conflicts in
discussions of distributive policy have become sharper
as well, so that the very real gains women have enjoyed
as beneficiaries of the policies of the progressive Swedish
welfare state may be in question. The absence of an organized feminist movement to press for continued commitment of social policies may be critical, although the
trend toward advocacy by joint groupings of women's
organizations from the different parties may lead to collective action on this front. To date, collective action has
been limited to "sexual" or "woman-specific" matters
(e.g., rape and pornography), which do not directly affect the parties' socioeconomic policy commitments.

Since 1976, of the two leftist parties, the VPK has been especially supportive of such issues as day care and the six-hour work day.* In 1985 over 80 percent of the VPK and about 70 percent of the SDP favored the building of more day-care centers and the six-hour workday.

Swedish surveys reveal that the concept of equal representation in Parliament for men and women has received little backing from any quarter. Principles loosely related to "affirmative action" are viewed with considerable apprehension by the Swedish public. Interestingly, given the state commitment to economic equality and independence for women, 46 percent of men and 48 percent of women in 1979 indicated that men should get jobs first. Another response that may signal difficulty ahead for the welfare state was the considerable support for reducing the public sector and social welfare commitment in 1982 and 1985. Prohibition of pornography, an issue initially supported by the more conservative parties, has come to reflect a dichotomy between male and female views. From 1979 to 1985 women consistently supported a ban in far greater numbers than men (in 1982, 51 percent of women, 28 percent of men; in 1985, 68 percent of women, 43 percent of men). There appears to be a growing awareness of this issue, which was highlighted by an all-women party demonstration in Stockholm. Eduards (1986) has noted that a majority of women (but not men) also favor the use of quotas to gain election to the Riksdag for women and oppose jobs for men first. (Some data also suggest a gender gap on the issue of abortion, with more women against [Eduards 1986; Sainsbury 1983]!) Whether these trends

*Attitudinal data for 1976–85 were made available by Soren Holmberg, University of Gothenburg.

augur a new feminist consciousness that may be translated into group activism is questionable, given the continued prevalence of norms related to Swedish political consensus within the corporate state. What is worth noting, however, is the apparent emergence of a separate female consciousness about some key women's concerns.

Opinion polls in the early 1980s found some contradictory responses to survey questions among the three nations (Hastings and Hastings 1985:707). Whereas 63 percent of Swedish respondents and 59 percent of American ones felt that men and women were treated equally, only 47 percent of British respondents thought so (and 40 percent replied that men were treated more favorably). Nonetheless, it is difficult to measure whether these data reflect a more truly egalitarian role for women in Swedish society or simply acceptance of the well-known institutionalized rhetoric. Table 13 presents a comparison of responses regarding 1) sexual equality in politics and 2) general customs and practices.

The data in the table indicate, perhaps somewhat surprisingly, that a far higher proportion of Swedish than American women perceive that equality has not been attained in politics or social life.

Table 13.
Attitudes Toward: (1) Politics;
(2) General Customs and Practices

Country	Men Treated More Favorably		Both Sexes Treated Equally	
United States	(1) 58%	(2) 20%	(1) 38%	(2) 70%
Sweden	(1) 78%	(2) 60%	(1) 15%	(2) 28%
United Kingdom	(1) 94%	(2) 71%	(1) 5%	(2) 22%

SOURCE: Adapted from Hastings and Hastings 1985:707–17.

Table 14.
*Distribution of Household Responsibilities
(in Percentage)*

	U.K.	U.S.
Household repairs:		
Done by men	76	39
Shared partially or equally	11	47
Cleaning house:		
Done by wife	66	46
Shared partially or equally	31	45
Cooking:		
Done by wife	73	55
Shared partially or equally	22	35

SOURCES: Hastings and Hastings 1982:239; 1983:285.

A crucial measure of egalitarian views is the distribution of household responsibilities (see Table 14).

In Sweden, despite the legal encouragement given to sexual equality, few husbands participate in child care, and other traditional sex roles appear to have remained entrenched. Thus, it appears that labor force participation per se has little impact on sharing of customary sex roles, particularly given the high incidence of part-time work among women, which is likely to reinforce existing patterns of domestic responsibility.

According to a 1976 study on Swedes at work by the Swedish Central Bureau of Statistics (cited in Scott 1982:78), in families where husband and wife were both employed *full time:*

67 percent of women did all or practically all the cooking;
50 percent did all or practically all the washing up;
80 percent did all the laundry;
53 percent did all or practically all the shopping; and
55 percent did all the cleaning.

As for the time spent by Swedish men who did "some" of the cleaning, shopping, cooking, and so on, a sample survey of 7,000 women made by the Committee on Equality in 1978 revealed that, overall (including families with women who were not employed full-time), men spent less than half as much time as women in daily routine household tasks. Sex segregation and "ubiquitous part-time work" have reinforced women's almost full responsibility for the household (Erickson and Aberg 1987:9).

Although the role of women in the domestic sphere still completely overshadows that of men, recent data demonstrate some movement toward leveling. From 1974 to 1981, men doubled their share of the family domestic responsibilities from a minute 7 percent to 14 percent. Differences between age groups are remarkably small and gender roles still very strong, although a larger percentage of men share household tasks with full-time working wives (Tahlin 1987:238). Recent Swedish survey data demonstrate that sex role differentiation in the home remains marked. Women are almost exclusively responsible for care of clothing (e.g., laundry, mending, and ironing). They are disproportionately involved in cooking, cleaning, and washing up and in child care as well (Equality Ministry 1985:57–58), while men engage in repair work, gardening, and car and boat maintenance.

Nonetheless, the distribution of household responsibilities reveals a more egalitarian division of labor between husbands and wives in Sweden and in the United States than in Britain, where, for instance, a larger majority of wives clean house. Similar patterns appear with regard to washing dishes, although in the United States, *children* are the most likely to help out (Hastings and Hastings 1985:712). American women are also the most likely to undertake such male-oriented tasks as gardening and lawn mowing (ibid.). (Nonetheless, in a recent survey of women only a fraction of U.S. respondents thought that real householding decision-making power was shared equally by both partners; and the Swedes were the fewest of all respondents to agree that males should be the major breadwinners and women should stay at home, which at least demonstrates the prevalence of the full-employment philosophy in Swedish culture [Hernes 1983:49].)

The data suggest that strong patterns of gender polarization and traditional sex role socialization persist even among the sons and daughters of the welfare state. Earlier we noted similar patterns discernible with regard to the taking of parental and sick leave. Data on political participation by women also demonstrate a continued separation between the public and private spheres among all socioeconomic classes in Sweden (Szulkin 1987:207–9), although the differences have narrowed somewhat in the last decade. However, union-meeting activity among women in Class I (primarily SACO/SR) and the proportion of women holding office in the LO declined from 1974 to 1981—perhaps a reflection of the increased growth of the part-time sector and lessened attachments to the workplace. Women's participation in corporate channels lagged behind men's by at least 10 percent. But data from the 1970s reveal decreasing gender differences in union and party activity and other efforts to influence the political process, especially in the 16–24 age group. Whether these patterns may continue to survive the demands of domestic responsibilities and counter prevalent trends in which males "out-participate" women is open to speculation (ibid., 201; Sainsbury 1983).

Clearly, support for some of feminism's basic goals,

including sex role modification, has met with great resistance not only in the more traditional United Kingdom but even in the "egalitarian" society that Sweden
has forged. In turn, as we have seen, the persistence of
traditional values has constrained political opportunities for feminists and, together with the rigid nature of
the political system, has limited their options. The British movement in particular has a long way to go in gaining support of women who do not enter into competi-
tion with men, and therefore do not feel unequal, and in
convincing the vast majority who are married, have
been married, or expect to be married that the feminist
movement they perceive as antimale is relevant to their
lives (Hills 1981:104).

Impact on Public Policy

Public policy reflecting feminist concerns has resulted
in Sweden, the United States, and Britain; in each of the
three nations, legislation on equal pay, sex discrimination, abortion, and domestic violence is in effect. However, the policy process both leading to and involving
implementation of legislation has been significantly different in each nation, thus influencing policy impact. In
the United States, policy has largely been the result of
lobbying by gender-based groups. As noted earlier, gender-based policy networks are made possible by the emphasis on coalition formation and the relative openness
of the political system to group participation.

Even though public policy in the United Kingdom on
such movement goals as equal pay, sex discrimination,
abortion, and domestic violence has reflected feminist
concerns (if not direct influence) via trade union and Labour Party politics, the impact of policy change has
been minimal. Some of the efforts made toward these

goals were prompted at least in part by EEC directives requiring equal pay and job equality. A major exception is in the area of abortion policy, where a coalition of trade unionists, feminists, and Labour Party activists has effectively intervened to prevent weakening of the existing law. (In addition to demonstrating against the Corrie Bill, in 1979, they mobilized after 1981 to lessen the impact of a restrictive interpretation of the Abortion Act by the DHSS that would limit circumstances in which doctors could perform abortions.) The EOC, TUC, and women's groups have also succeeded in expanding public consciousness about such issues as positive action and "equal value" (pay equity) (Atkins and Hoggett 1984:198). In Britain the continued efforts by such activists as the women's rights officer of the NCCL (since 1975), increased strength in white-collar unions like the NUPE (where training courses and baby-sitting services have been established for working women, with a resultant increase in the number of shop stewards and TUC delegates) (Vallance 1985:30), as well as efforts at the local council level provide evidence of ongoing attempts to achieve policy change. However, whereas in both the United Kingdom and the United States it has been more difficult to secure policy implementation than the legislation itself, in the United States opportunities for intervention in bureaucratic politics are far greater.

In Britain, owing to ideological purism and localized structures, women have not developed political networks comparable to those in the United States. Institutional factors such as the growth of administrative power and executive dominance and secrecy, combined with the strength of parties and Parliament, have limited opportunities for direct intervention in policy-making and made monitoring of implementation well-nigh impossible. The women's liberation movement's emphasis on "women-specific" issues, such as abortion, rape, and domestic violence, while of utmost importance, has sometimes obscured the significance of issues involving work and the family ("organization of daily life" issues) so crucial to change for women.

When the Conservative government came to power in 1979, the tone was one of de-legitimization of women's right to work, as exemplified by the opinions of Lord Spens who, opening a debate on unemployment, said that married women should leave paid employment to make way for men (Huws 1985:57). Shortly thereafter, this view was reinforced by Thatcher's secretary of state for social services, who contended that women should look after their children full time and that state aid be restricted to very needy cases. As noted in Chapter 1, state provision of nursery and child care has never been adequate in Britain, and when other benefits were also cut, stipends to dependent mothers and children became even more meager. These events were not greeted with any mass response by the feminist movement in Britain.

In contrast, the positive changes in laws relating to violence against women were in part a response to women's campaigns, although these were often marked by the feminist ambivalence and the inaccessibility to the political system, as discussed earlier. As van der Gaag (1985:137) has correctly pointed out, Women's Aid never perceived legislation as particularly important in altering women's position in society and in the family. Nonetheless, feminists did intervene when they pushed for the Housing (Homeless) Persons Act of 1977, which gave priority in local housing to women who fled their homes because of violence. They also campaigned for changing the law on injunctions, discussed earlier. But there have been massive difficulties with enforcement in the face of a hostile judiciary and police force and the feminists' inability to monitor implementation (Williscroft 1985:103). Sums made available to the shelter movement by local and central government grants have been minimal, for the same reasons.

Similar difficulties have ensued with regard to the Sexual Offences (Amendment) Act dealing with rape. Funding problems and failures of enforcement and interpretation remain. British feminists have concluded that the act has appreciably affected neither the way in which trials are conducted nor their reporting. Williscroft (ibid.) concludes that legislation at the local and national level has been of marginal importance. The failure of legislation to produce significant gains may result in either political quiescence or heightened cynicism regarding the political process, reinforcing the isolation of British feminists in any case.

We have argued that though the Sex Discrimination Act and the Equal Pay Act were potentially important pieces of legislation, they have not been implemented effectively enough to challenge inequality. The absence of coalitions and the failure to create a feminist infrastructure that might transcend ideological differences have been crucial. These deficiencies have to some degree been averted in the United States, where affirmative action practices are much more widely practiced than in Britain, reflecting a major difference between the American EEOC and the British EOC created by the Sex Discrimination Act (Dex and Shaw 1986:4). Affirmative action is viewed with suspicion and hostility in a Britain dominated by high unemployment and economic strain, while in the United States, women have benefitted from more vigorous implementation of equal opportunity and affirmative action directives.

Three factors account for more effective enforcement of sex discrimination laws in the United States than in Britain or Sweden: 1) legislative and judicial commitment to the principle of affirmative action or positive discrimination, including the use of sanctions against offenders; 2) greater public acceptance of and mobilization for affirmative action principles; and 3) monitoring and intervention by a feminist network. In addition, the range of legislation that the EEOC can call on is impressive, as are the resources at its disposal, particularly in comparison with the United Kingdom and Sweden. The EEOC employs 3,100 people in a Washington office and 48 district or local offices (Grant 1984:52). It is thus far more accessible to the public than the minute British office (170 employees, primarily in Manchester, in 1984) and the even tinier Swedish version (7 employees). Federal guidelines appear to have produced significant gains in hiring and promotion in companies that do business with government, particularly if supported by vigorous organization and litigation (Law 1988:31, 33).

The American tradition of litigation for equal rights has provided a securer foundation for equality than has the British approach, even in a period of conservative rule. There has been less erosion in the U.S. public policy arena because it has been buttressed by strong public support for affirmative action (64 percent in 1984) (Hastings and Hastings 1985:541), the concept of "indirect discrimination," the ability to bring class action suits (minimizing individual costs and providing relief to large numbers), a professional feminist litigation sector, and continual feminist lobbying and networking. As Grant has found, there is extraordinary support among

American business for the practice of affirmative action, in part because this provides far more utilization of human resources and opens the workplace to new talent and ideas (Grant 1984:60). Unlike the unions in Britain and Sweden that opposed national legislation against sex discrimination and remain lukewarm toward it today, in the United States the initially hostile business community strongly supports the continuation of aggressive federal affirmative action and equal opportunity guidelines.

In particular, the employment of black women, especially in firms with federal contracts, increased significantly as a result of EEOC policies. The major impact of equal opportunity policy has been at the professional and managerial level. It is at this level, as we shall see, that American women have achieved gains that exceed those made by women in Sweden and Britain (Dex and Shaw 1986:224).

It is undeniable that because of the largesse of the Swedish welfare state, benefits to single-female heads of families, to female members of the labor force, and to their children are far superior to those offered in the United States and Britain. Over 50 percent of Swedish children were in child-care facilities funded and regulated by the government in 1980, but only 15 percent of American children were similarly advantaged in 1984 (although a large number of American women relied on private-sector group and individual day care, bringing overall coverage to about the same level) (Bianchi and Spahn 1986:230). While 40 percent of American women have maternity coverage through their employment, 76 percent of Swedish women have that benefit (through the state) (Jonung 1984:50). Generous family rent and maintenance allowances, paid parental and sick leaves, in addition to special subsidies for single parents, have created a system that provides a far higher standard of living, without stigmatization and without long-term dependency and work disincentives, than in the United States (Kamerman 1984).

Swedish parties have proven receptive to women's sections' views on such issues as day care and leaves, but in fact the inception of many of these issues predates an active role for women's groups. Because the unions and parties sought to discourage further economic inclusion of immigrant groups, the participation of women in the labor force was encouraged in the 1960s. Policies related to women were therefore not informed by a feminist perspective, although they clearly sought to create equal opportunity for all, primarily through full employment. Both the SDP and the powerful unions, especially the LO, have opposed state intervention in order to strengthen institutional guarantees against sexual discrimination and have continued to view voluntary agreements between labor and employers as more significant than legislation. As we have noted, "equality" policies on sex discrimination and on lack of employment opportunities for women met with a tepid response from the unions and Social Democrats, so that these policies have been narrowly defined and limited to employment-related issues. Given their lukewarm attitude, there has been scant impetus to gain compliance with anti-sex discrimination efforts through the effective application of government policy since the resumption of political power by the Social Democrats and their labor allies in 1982. At present, in an atmosphere in which the dominant political view is that "equality" already exists, women's sections within the four parties that have them appear to be playing a quiescent role. Though in the past they provided women with an opportunity to voice their special concerns, today women's sections may "ghettoize" participation and prevent fuller inclusion in decision-making.

In the main, women lack independent resources with which to seek further implementation and discussion of their concerns, including intransigent issues such as part-time work, occupational segregation, and limited mobility. We have seen that Sweden represents a society in which women have been politically incorporated without being fully mobilized; so their demands as claimants in the political system have been dealt with by the male-dominated corporatist power structure on its terms. Women, unlike men, have been unable to create a basis for organization in the labor market owing to their lesser numbers and representation and to the active discouragement of women's groups in the labor force. Nor have they effectively created independent groups related to other aspects of their lives.

Despite Sweden's official policies mandating change in men's roles as well as women's, absence from work because of child-care needs is almost exclusively restricted to women. Nearly eight out of ten men transfer their parental leave to women (mothers), and family life is organized so that women work part-time in order to care for children and home. Work, society, and politics are still organized on patriarchal lines despite the existence of "equal opportunity" (Equality Ministry 1985: 11, 79–83).

Policies concerning what we may call the "organization of daily life" (e.g., child care and parental leave) have proven costly and difficult to implement in the absence of a significant movement continuously advocating for them. The result: Sweden remains highly sex-segregated in politics, work, and the home. In the absence of a feminist frame of reference, women's issues have been subsumed under "equality" and "family policy" and no longer regarded as a problem. Women-only issues involving "sexual" or "body" concerns have been belatedly recognized and incorporated into state policy mechanisms; they are treated as minor problems despite their relatively high incidence in a society viewed as violence-free. The fact that a grass-roots voluntary movement has arisen with regard to wife abuse indicates that the pervasiveness of male violence against women is a key social issue even in consensus-oriented Sweden. Similarly, the emerging differences on such issues as affirmative action for women may demonstrate increased consciousness of feminist concerns among Swedish women.

Swedish women have in fact not really left their homes; their major domestic responsibilities and very partial attachment to the labor force (to be discussed further) has resulted in the continuing primacy of traditional sex roles and society. The socialization of traditional women's roles in public-sector paid employment and the existence of benefits that help support women's part-time status may reinforce rather than change sex roles over the long run.

In examining the Swedish policy process, it seems clear that Swedish unions and parties have "literally preempted feminist demands and have put their political clout behind numerous proposals to advance equality between women and men" (Scott 1982:53). Enactment of public policy has in large measure left the unions and parties free to pursue issues of equality in the workplace and in their own decision-making bodies at their own pace and on their own terms, and issues of power sharing and male dominance have largely been left untouched. As Verba and Orren (1985:130–31) point out, the SDP has worked "deliberately and successfully to make gender equality a subset of the general issue of equality and not a separate, isolated set of demands. . . . In Sweden, the Social Democrats . . . shaped feminist demands; in the United States feminist demands transformed the Democrats."

We have indicated that the issue of wife beating and abuse, identified in the American context as the more neutral policy arena known as "domestic violence," illustrates a good deal about the nature of the American political process and the receptivity of the system to feminist issues. Although the shelter movement began in England and exists belatedly in Sweden as well, it has been most successful in a number of ways in the American setting. The creation of shelters under the aegis of feminist groups legitimized the issue as a policy agenda matter, and by 1982 there were at least 300 shelters (plus hundreds of "safe houses") in operation (Pleck 1987:199).

Coalitions were created to combat treatment of battered women in 48 states. State funds became available, largely owing to pressure from shelter staff and residents, as well as other coalition members. Federal aid was forthcoming from a variety of sources, although it was not until 1984 that federal funding ($6 million) was finally appropriated for shelter support specifically, after several years of strident attacks from the New Right, which feared what was perceived as the weakening of the nuclear family. Since 1985, Congress has appropriated additional funding for shelters, and several additional federal programs have come to the aid of victims of domestic violence. In almost every state as well, laws have been enacted to improve reporting procedures, mandate police intervention, and establish more effective criminal court procedures (ibid., 192–98). As Pleck (ibid., 199) points out, the process of gaining legitimization for intervention in domestic violence meant some dilution of the original radical feminist ideas that gave rise to the shelter movement. The inclusive coalitions involved in pushing for reform were often pressed to compromise because of the broad-based nature of the movement as it developed strength. Thus, a price was paid for success in gaining funding, legislation, and new legal enforcement: feminist rhetoric and control of shelters and even the movement's direction were affected. Nonetheless, the conclusion reached in this analysis is that the new coalition spurred by autonomous feminist movements allied with legislators, the judicial enforcement process, and other activists, including the social work profession, produced gains that made domestic violence a priority issue and helped achieve significant change. Women as claimants in this policy arena have had considerable success, and the diffusion of feminist ideas into the political culture seems evident.

The reluctance of British feminists to engage the national political system on the issue of battered women provides a clear contrast. The ready co-optation by the Swedish political system of the issue, at the same time as it was placed on the policy agenda, may have muted the important process of conflict and controversy, leaving in question both the fate of the grass-roots voluntary efforts that helped raise the issue initially and the vigor of the implementation process in the absence of an autonomous feminist movement (Lundqvist 1980:196).

In the United States the existence of numerous channels to influence policy—the executive, the courts, the states, and the legislature—may facilitate the diffusion of issues at different levels and permit pressure to initiate and enforce policy. We therefore contend that the relatively permeable American political system permits more choices than that of Britain or Sweden for change-oriented groups such as feminists and helps provide numerous reinforcements for the activity of independently organized and funded groups. Even though the policy process is characterized by incrementalism, with regard to a once "radical" issue such as wife abuse or domestic violence, it seems quite responsive to demands for change.

Changing Economic Roles for Women

A final area for examination is the significance of women's increased presence in the labor force as a vehicle for personal and societal change. Two different types of public policies must be considered to understand the increased mobility of American, as opposed to Swedish, women. Policies of the first type *facilitate* labor force participation—these are the policies provided much more generously by the Swedish state than by the American one. Policies of the second type foster greater economic opportunity by *expanding* the possibilities and choices available to women. In this second arena, characterized by commitment to affirmative action and widespread feminist consciousness, the United States (and even Britain, with a longer and somewhat more meaningful commitment to equal opportunity enactments) appears to have surpassed Sweden.

In Chapter 1 it was shown that women's labor force participation in each of the three nations discussed has increased phenomenally during the post-World War II

Table 15.
*Part-Time Employment
of Women and Men*

Country	Women	Men
Sweden	46.2%	7.3%
United Kingdom	42.4%	3.3%
United States	23.3%	7.6%

SOURCE: Equality Ministry 1985:12.

period and continues to grow annually in each nation. In 1983, 58 percent of British women, 61 percent of American women, and 77 percent of Swedish women were employed (Equality Ministry 1985:12). Nonetheless, although the employment of Swedish women was the highest of all three, so was the percentage of women employed part-time (see Table 15). As Erikson and Aberg (1987:9) have pointed out, "It is to part-time work in the public sector that newly employed [Swedish] women have moved. Women are overrepresented in unqualified work, have little independence at the job, and are underrepresented in supervisory positions. Both sex segregation and the ubiquitous part-time work are the reasons for their low income."

In the United Kingdom and Sweden, women are disproportionately employed by the public service sector, and there they are increasingly employed in part-time positions (Dex and Shaw 1986:122). In Sweden, 90 percent of the women who work do so in the service sector, a vast majority being employed by the government, in contrast to about 75 percent in the United States and Britain (Mailler and Ross 1987:34–35; Hernes 1984:32). Forty-five percent of all women were employed in the social welfare sector in Sweden, 28 percent in the United States, and 26 percent in England. As Rein (1985 : 46) and others have shown, the social welfare sector is also the most highly segregated, with Sweden and Britain having the highest patterns of sex segregation (82 percent and 76 percent, respectively) and the United States the lowest (66 percent).

Occupational segregation is a problem in all three countries, but probably the greatest amount of change can be discerned in the United States, where there has been a decrease in occupational segregation and downward mobility after childbirth (Dex and Shaw 1986: 80–107; Bianchi and Spahn 1986:182). In Sweden, especially, occupational choice has been very much an extension of the traditional role of women (i.e., child care and service roles), and sex segregation remains a persistent problem.

Another obstinate problem affecting women's role and power is that of wage differentials between men and women, in large measure a function of part-time work and occupational segregation. In Britain, women's hourly earnings were 74 percent of men's, while gross earnings were 61 percent whereas in the United States they were 83 percent and 65 percent, respectively. Among American women ages 26 to 34 this gap has narrowed to 75 percent of men's income, and for ages 20 to 24 it has narrowed even further to about 86 percent (*New York Times,* Feb. 6, 1987: D2; Coote and Campbell 1987:18; EOC 1983a: 89; *Money,* Dec. 1986:62). In Sweden, full-time female workers earned about 80 percent of male income, but because of the large part-time component of work force, total female earnings are in fact about half of men's (Eduards 1981:210).

A significant measure of the economic role of Swedish, British, and American women is the disparity between women in each country who hold managerial and supervisory positions. Even accounting for differences in data-gathering methodology, the differences are striking. In contrast to the United States, in which over 35 percent of managers and administrators are female, the comparable numbers in the United Kingdom and Scandinavia are 18.8 and 11–15 percent (Davidson 1985:91). In Sweden, women occupy only 0.2 percent of the managerial positions (men occupy 7 percent), 3 percent of executive positions, and less than 1 percent of the top positions in companies and public authorities (Equality Ministry 1985:20). Four percent of the senior government executives and officials are women. In the United States the female share of executive, administrative, and managerial jobs rose from 20 percent in 1972 to 35 percent in 1985, almost doubling (Bergmann 1986:68). The United Kingdom occupies a middle position: women slightly decreased their role as managers in 1983 and now hold 17 percent of the administrative and professional positions (EOC 1983a:97). However, in the private sector in 1986, women held only 0.3 percent of the top positions in companies and only six percent of senior managerial posts (EOC 1987:2; *New York Times*, May 6, 1987: C1). British women hold 18.5 percent of appointments to public bodies, but are only 2 percent of the directorates of private sector firms. Only 25 women are found among the top three grades of the senior civil service (of 658) and only nine women among the boards of the hundred largest companies, while in the United States, 36 percent of corporate boardrooms had female members in 1982 (*New York Times*, May 6, 1987: C1; *Economist*, Nov. 1, 1986:58; Cooper 1985:16). Hernes (1983:17) shows that British women held from 8 to 12 percent of the country's top administrative positions, whereas in Scandinavia in general and Sweden in par-

Table 16.
Occupational Stratification

Occupational category	U.K.		Sweden		U.S.	
	M	F	M	F	M	F
High-prestige professional and technical	4.8	2.3	8.5	6.2	11.1	6.7
Administrative and managerial	6.1	0.9	5.2	0.4	10.4	3.0

SOURCE: Roos 1985: Table 3.3.

ticular no more than 2 percent of the top managers were women.

A comparative analysis of occupational stratification of women in Britain, Sweden, and the United States suggests trends similar to those described here (see Table 16).

Although strict comparability is not possible because of the absence of incisive cross-national data, the available data reveal that "professional employment [has] widened more rapidly and significantly in the United States, as females have during the last generation made serious inroads into a wide range of professional occupations" (Mailler and Ross 1987:46). Although this quotation refers specifically only to Britain and the United States, our analysis indicates that the Swedish case may demonstrate greater resistance to women, particularly in senior administrative and managerial roles. The virtual absence of women in such positions in Sweden may be attributable to women's marginal attachment to the labor force—owing both to occupational segregation and to part-time work, which continually reinforces the role of women as responsible for the domestic sphere—and Swedish cultural norms that appear to decry assertive, individualistic women as beyond the pale of consensus politics.

The pattern of higher education in each country buttresses the economic role of women. In Sweden, although 66 percent of university graduates in 1982–83 were women, postgraduate work was dominated by men (Equality Ministry 1985:34). (In 1986, only 23 percent of postgraduate students were women, down from 27 percent in 1982.) The proportion of female university students is largest in the United States, and they now reap more than half of the bachelor's and master's degrees and one-third of the doctoral degrees awarded (*New York Times*, Feb. 6, 1987: D2). In the more elitist British educational system, 5 percent of women held bachelor's or advanced degrees, whereas in the United States the number was 20 percent (Dex and Shaw 1986:34).

Women in all three countries have greatly improved their representation in medicine. (Is it perceived as an extension of the "caring" role?) The high number of Swedish female dentists (34 percent) is particularly notable (*Statistical Abstract* 1987). However, in the United States, 11 percent of engineers are women, in the United Kingdom only 3 percent, while in Sweden women hold about 5 percent of construction-related positions (a category including architects and engineers) (ibid.; Tomes 1985:77). Only 10 percent of American women planned to major in education in 1985; business was now the most popular undergraduate major for both men and women. The proportion of M.B.A.'s awarded to women rose from 3 percent in 1965 to 30 percent in 1986 (Bianchi and Spahn 1986:119). American women have made particular strides in the field of law, where they earned 38 percent of degrees awarded, up from 15 percent in 1975 (*New York Times,* Feb. 6, 1987: D2). In Britain, 11 percent of the barristers in 1983 were women (a number that rose to 17 percent toward the end of the decade) and 14 percent of the solicitors (Williscroft 1985: 100). In Sweden, about 11 percent of lawyers and jurists are women (*Statistical Abstract* 1987); in the United States, almost 20 percent.

American women compose 27 percent of university faculties and about 12 percent of all professors; in Britain, female professors number less than 4 percent (*Economist,* Aug. 23, 1986: 14; "Equality Between Men and Women" 1987). In 1982, 5 percent of Swedish women were professors (*Chronicle of Higher Education,* Sept. 10, 1986: 26; Tomes 1985: 74).

The contrast between the growing economic and professional gains of American women and to a lesser degree, their British sisters, seems to highlight continued inequities in Sweden. While as many Swedish women as men interviewed by a survey said they would like to be promoted, only 5 percent thought they would be (Equality Ministry 1985: 20). Through the division of labor, then, Swedish "men are able to preserve a dominant, superior position. Men still occupy practically all positions conferring power and influence in society. . . . Women do not compete with men because they live on different terms" (ibid., 79).

Assessment

In this analysis we have argued that structural factors, including political, cultural, and economic constraints, narrow the possibilities for women to become policy claimants. We have marshaled evidence to demonstrate the importance of women articulating on behalf of their own interests and own concerns, contending that the "strident" tones of women's liberation decried by some are a necessary, if not sufficient, condition for societal change (Hewlett 1986:166).

A causal relationship between movement politics, policy enactments, and the growth of a professionally active group of women with economic and political potential is not fully demonstrable, but it is evident that the American feminist movement has had a profound impact on changing expectations and possibilities. In 1984, 49 percent of the women surveyed by *Ms* magazine (July 1984:54) indicated that they would continue to work even if they did not have to do so for economic reasons, while 57 percent indicated that they felt the "women's movement has just begun." The evidence of the continued vigor of the American feminist movement seems fairly conclusive, suggesting that reports of its demise are premature and unfounded.

This analysis has stressed the significance of several major factors that appear to limit the role of British feminists: the closed and inflexible nature of British government, particularly the administrative process; the reluctance of key institutions such as parties and unions to go beyond rhetoric in meaningfully sharing power; and the localized, purist nature of the women's liberation movement, which has failed to create coalitions and an enduring national presence. In Sweden, the anomaly of progressive policies pertaining to women, despite the lack of an independent, feminist movement, has resulted in a set of political contradictions. Notwithstanding the greater hospitableness of the Swedish party system in particular to pressure, in practice the system permits little ideological or political space for nonproducer groups. Issues drawn from the feminist agenda have found their way into the public policy arena and have profoundly influenced expectations, particularly regarding women's role as labor force participants. But in the absence of an autonomous independent movement that could structure dialogue on its own terms, much of the policy enacted appears to have had little impact on gender-based roles. The continued existence of a huge part-time female work force, the extraordinarily high degree of labor force segregation based on sex, and the apparent persistence of traditional sex roles imply that the general labor force policy that benefits women is not enough.

This analysis has sought to demonstrate the interaction between the "political opportunity structures" and mobilization by feminist social movements. In turn, the product of this interaction has affected the success of feminist claims and the degree of social change possible in each nation. Although the concept of success utilized here has emphasized policy outcomes, it has not neglected other manifestations, such as movement survival, changes in individual consciousness, and diffusion of group values. The results of these developments include acceptance of the group as a legitimate political organization, with ensuing gains for its members.

We have argued that policy impact may often rely on implementation efforts by a coalition of feminists and their political allies, and that the efforts may best succeed if these feminists are members of autonomous groupings that enjoy access to the political process, as is the case in the United States. American feminists also seem to have achieved the most public support for movement goals and ideals, now broadly diffused throughout the culture. With regard to individual consciousness, we contend that feminist ideology has had a profound impact on women in all three nations, although it has sprung from different sources. In the context of its self-defined goals British nondirected "liberationist" movement politics is remarkable for its continued vigor and survival. In his analysis of social movements and policy change, Tarrow (1983:8) has observed that "the range and flexibility of its tactical repertory is often a good predictor of movement success." We have contended that the American movement has enjoyed the greatest autonomy in choice of tactics because it has been unconstrained by the necessity to work through the intermediation of existing groups, such as parties and unions. This freedom has permitted the use of a variety of tactics from protest to participation in existing power groupings. British feminist participation has been constrained by the rigidity of the political system and the ambivalence of movement activists about engaging in national politics in a coordinated fashion. Swedish women have, in the main, been limited to behaving as participants in existing institutions.

In all three nations, the relatively unstable nature of traditional electoral coalitions and the declining relationship between unions and the working class have produced new opportunities for women as potential recruits and bases of strength. In Sweden and the United States, these new opportunities appear to have produced the most responsiveness to new policies for women, although they have created different results. The crucial factor appears to be the greater availability of allies or coalition partners in these two countries. In the United States in the last two decades, relationships have been cemented between feminists, other like-minded groups, and the Democratic Party, while in Sweden electoral instability created new opportunities for political access for women, particularly in the 1970s.

As Tarrow (ibid., 45) puts it, political "reforms may be more reversible when they are substantive only, creating no new vested rights of participation or veto in the population groups newly enjoying them." This hypothesis argues, then, for the idea that reforms producing institutionalized participation may be the most significant of all, largely because they help create resources for future mobilization and ensure continued attention to substantive policy concerns. Seen from this perspective, the American movement, now recognized as a legitimate group in the pluralist system, may be in the strongest position to endure as a significant political force.

From the examination of substantive policy gains, this analysis has found that Americans have achieved the most in expanding economic opportunities, while the Swedes have been most successful in creating a support structure that facilitates female labor force participation. Substantive rights, such as access to equal employment, are, as we have seen, limited by support from government and willingness to use sanctions, the sympathetic response of the public and political allies, and continued intervention by an activist feminist policy network. Legislation, it appears, is not enough, as it is necessary to have continued access to the implementation process in order to consolidate policy gains and achieve further political success. In the final analysis, all three nations demonstrate the limitations of their "political opportunity structure" as it affects the role of women. In the case of Sweden, gender-neutral policies have not yet been able to encompass the special needs and experiences of women and liberate them from their traditional roles. And, in the United States and in Britain despite the strength of the independent feminist tradition that has acted from a collective position in the name of collective goals, individual women have been forced to struggle with family responsibilities still squarely rooted in the private sphere.

Methodological Appendix

The material on Britain presented in this book is the result of three visits there: in spring 1980 and the summers of 1982 and 1984. The research in Sweden was conducted in summer 1986. Analysis of American feminism is based on research done from 1980 to 1986 for an earlier book, *Women and Public Policies*, and an article, "The Politics of Wife Abuse." In each country, research was based primarily on interviews with feminist scholars and activists, as well as women active in political parties, unions, and civic groups and women in elective and appointive political positions. The period studied covers the 1960s through the mid-1980s.

This book is based on both written and interview data, which are listed in the bibliography that follows.* The semistructured interviews were held with activists in various segments of the women's movement, as well as women journalists, politicians, and administrative officials. Each interview lasted from one to three hours; several people were seen more than once. In each country, academics, primarily either in sociology or in political science, were extremely helpful in providing an overview and initial list of prospective contacts. Names of possible interviewees were also derived from news-

---

*No interviews are listed for U.S. women because those interviews, as I've noted, were conducted for other published work during the period 1980–86.

papers and from government and other publications. Most importantly, names were constantly checked with those interviewed. Although this sample does not purport to be "scientifically" representative of the women's movement in Britain, Sweden, and the United States, I believe that, within the constraints of time and availability, I was able to touch base with representatives of all relevant groups. Almost 100 women with ties to the women's movement were interviewed specifically for this project in the United Kingdom and Sweden; in the United States, as a result of research for a book, several articles, and a monograph, an equal number were reached. Inevitably, points made in interviews were counterchecked with other interviewees and in the documentary and journalistic literature as well.

Because this study is based primarily on research at the national level, it reflects a bias toward national policy-making, although in England I sought particularly to talk with several women who represented new trends at the local level. Even in England, however, the focus was London, and not other urban (nor rural) areas. In Sweden and the United States, attention centered on the capital cities of Stockholm and Washington, D.C., owing to the research focus. In many ways, the interviews provided the major core of the research, but they were also validated and reinforced by numerous other resources. Interviews were thus used to stimulate inquiry, gain data, learn about unfamiliar issues and politics (especially abroad), and check information gleaned from other sources, including other interviews and written materials.

Inevitably, there are hazards in making international comparisons based on data that are often collected in different ways. So the process of doing comparative research, while extraordinarily rewarding, is also very difficult. I have relied particularly on data supplied by each nation's statistics, although in the case of Britain this effort was complicated by the fact that the British Annual Abstract of Statistics does not classify economic activity by sex in the same manner as the other nations. In addition, I have utilized cross-national data whenever possible, a task made more complex because the meaning of such classifications as "executive" is often undefined. I have made every effort to analyze comparative data with care, given the limitations of collection, definition, and interpretation.

Bibliography

Books and Articles

Adams, Carolyn, and Katherine Winston. 1980. *Mothers at Work.* New York: Longman.

Adlam, Diana. 1980. "Socialist Feminism and Contemporary Politics." In *Politics and Power #1: New Perspectives on Socialist Politics.* London: Routledge and Kegan Paul.

Allerbuck, Klaus, M. Kent Jennings, and Leopold Rosenmayr. 1979. "Generations and Families." In *Political Action: Mass Participation in Five Western Democracies,* edited by S. Barnes and Max Kaase, 487–522. Beverly Hills, Calif.: Sage.

Annual Abstract of Statistics, Britain. 1986–1988. London: Her Majesty's Stationery Office.

Anton, Thomas J. 1969. "Policy Making and Political Culture in Sweden." *Scandinavian Political Studies* 4:88–102.

———. 1980. *Administered Politics: Elite Political Culture in Sweden.* Hingham, Mass.: Kluwer Academic.

Ashford, Douglas. 1981. *Policy and Politics in Britain.* Philadelphia: Temple University Press.

Anim, Bonnie. 1986. "Class Structure: Five-Country Comparative Data." Department of Sociology, University of Wisconsin.

Atkins, Susan, and Brenda Hoggett. 1984. *Women and the Law.* Oxford: Basil Blackwell.

Banks, Olive. 1981. *Faces of Feminism.* New York: St. Martin's Press.

Barnes, Samuel, and Max Kaase. 1979. *Political Action: Mass Participation in Western Democracies.* Beverly Hills, Calif.: Sage.

Barrett, Michelle. 1980. *Women's Oppression Today.* London: Verso.

Bassnett, Susan. 1986. *Feminist Experiences: The Women's Movement in Four Cultures.* London: Allen and Unwin.

Baude, Annika. 1979. *Public Policy and Changing Family Patterns in Sweden, 1930–77.* Stockholm: Swedish Center for Working Life, National Board of Welfare.

Bell, Deborah. 1985. "Unionized Women in State and Local Government." In *Women, Work and Protest,* edited by Ruth Milkman, 280–99. Boston: Routledge and Kegan Paul.

Beloff, Max, and Gillian Peele. 1980. *The Government of the United Kingdom: Political Authority in a Changing Society.* London: William Field and Nicholason.

Bergmann, Barbara. 1986. *The Economic Emergence of Women.* New York: Basic Books.

Bianchi, Suzanne, and Daphne Spahn. 1986. *American Women in Transition.* New York: Russell Sage Foundation.

Bjorklund, Anders. 1984. "A Look at Male-Female Unemployment Differentials in the Federal Republic of Germany, Sweden, U.K. and U.S.A." In *Sex Discrimination and Equal Opportunity,* edited by Gunther Schmid and Renate Weitzel, 220–43. New York: St. Martin's Press.

Blondel, Jean. 1974. *Voters, Parties and Leaders.* London: Penguin.

Boles, Janet. 1984. "The Texas Woman in Politics: Role Model or Mirage?" *Social Science Journal,* January, 77–90.

Bomafede, Dom. 1986. "Still a Long Way to Go." *National Journal* 13 (September): 2175–79.

Boneparth, Ellen. 1984. "Women and Public Policies: Comparative Perspectives on Welfare Mothers." In *Public Policy and Social Institutions,* edited by Harrell Rodgers, 127–53. Greenwich, Conn.: JAI Press.

Bouchier, David. 1984. *The Feminist Challenge: The Movement for Women's Liberation in Britain and the United States.* New York: Schocken Books.

Braun, Rachel. 1984. "Equal Opportunity and the Law in the U.S." In *Sex Discrimination and Equal Opportunity,* edited by Gunther Schmid and Renate Weitzel, 92–106. New York: St. Martin's Press.

Breitenbach, Esther. 1981. "A Comparative Study of the Women's Trade Union Conference and the Scottish Women's TUC." *Feminist Review* 8 (Spring): 65–86.

Brimelow, Elizabeth. 1981. "Women in the Civil Service." *Public Administration* 59 (Autumn): 313–35.

Bruegel, Irene. 1983. "Women's Employment, Legislation and the Labour Market." In *Women's Welfare/Women's Rights,* edited by Jane Lewis, 80–169. London: Croom Helm.

Bunch, Charlotte. 1981. "Beyond Either/Or Feminist Options" and "The Reform Tool Kit." In *Building Feminist Theory: Essays from Quest,* edited by Quest Staff, 44–56, 189–201. New York: Longman.

Bureau of Labor Statistics. 1983. *Time for Change: 1983 Handbook for Women Workers.* Washington, D.C.

Butler, David, and Dennis Kavanaugh. 1984. *The Election of 1983.* London: Macmillan.

Byrne, Paul, and Joni Lovenduski. 1978a. "The Equal Opportunities Commission." *Women's Studies International Quarterly* 1:131–67.

———. 1978b. "Sex Equality and the Law in Britain." *British Journal of Law and Society* 5(2): 148–65.

Callendar, Claire. 1985. "Gender, Inequality and Social Policy." *Journal of Social Policy* 14:189–213.

Carroll, Susan. 1984. "The Recruitment of Women for Cabinet Level Posts in State Government: A Social Control Perspective." *Social Science Journal,* January, 1–91.

Central Statistics. 1986. *Kvinno-och Mansvarlden.* Stockholm: Central Statistics.

"Child Care Programs in Sweden." 1984. *Facts Sheets on Sweden.* Stockholm: Swedish Institute. September.

Christoph, James P. 1974. "Capital Punishment and British Politics: The Role of Pressure Groups." In *Pressure Groups in Britain: A Reader,* edited by Richard Kember and J. J. Richardson, 143–49. London: Dent.

Coalition of Labor Union Women, Center for Research and Education. 1980. "Absent from the Agenda: A Report on the Role of Women in American Unions." New York. Mimeo.

Colon, Rose. 1982. "A Practical Resource Guide to the Women's Movement in Sweden." Stockholm: By the Author.

Conover, Patricia, and Virginia Gray. 1984. *Feminism and the New Right*. New York: Praeger.

Cook, Alice. 1979. "Working Women: European Experience and American Need." In *Women in the U.S. Labor Force*, edited by Ann Foote Cahn, 271–306. New York: Praeger.

Cook, Alice, and Roberta Till Ritz. 1981. "Labor Education and Women Workers: An International Comparison." In *Labor Education for Women Workers*, edited by Barbara Wertheimer, 255–65. Philadelphia: Temple University Press.

Cooper, Gary. 1985. "Positive Action for Female Executives." *Women in Management Review* 1, no. 1 (Spring): 15–19.

Coote, Anna, and Beatrix Campbell. 1987. *Sweet Freedom: The Struggle for Women's Liberation*. 2d ed. Oxford: Basil Blackwell.

Coote, Anna, and Tess Gill. 1979. *Battered Women and the New Laws*. Guide No. 1. London: National Council for Civil Liberties.

Coote, Anna, and Peter Kellner. 1981. "Hear This, Brother: Women Workers and Union Power." *New Statesman*, 8–11.

Costain, Anne. 1982. "Representing Women." In *Women, Power and Policy*, edited by Ellen Boneparth, 19–37. Elmsford, N.Y.: Pergamon.

Coultas, Valerie. 1981. "Feminists Must Face the Future." *Feminist Review*, no. 7: 30–40.

Curtis, R. L., and L. Zurcher. 1974. "Social Movements." *Social Problems* 21: 356–70.

Dahlerup, Drude, and Brita Gulli. 1985. "Women's Organizations in the Nordic Countries" and "Summary." In *Unfinished Democracy: Women in Nordic Politics*, edited by Elina Haavio-Mannila et al., 6–36, 160–69. Elmsford, N.Y.: Pergamon Press.

Daniel, W. W. 1980. "Women's Experiences of Maternity Rights." *Gazette* (Legislation Department of Employment) 88 (May): 468–71.

David, Miriam. 1983. "The New Right Education and Social Policy." In *Women's Welfare/Women's Rights*, edited by Jane Lewis, 193–218. London: Croom Helm.

Davidson, Marilyn J. 1985. "Women Managers: The Present and Future." *Women in Management Review* 1, no. 2 (Summer): 91–94.

Deckard, Barbara S. 1983. *The Women's Movement.* New York: Harper and Row.

Dex, Shirley, and Lois B. Shaw. 1986. *British and American Women at Work: Do Equal Opportunities Policies Matter?* New York: St. Martin's Press.

Dobash, R. Emerson, and Russell Dobash. 1984. "The Response of the British and American Women's Movements to Violence Against Women." In *Women, Violence, and Social Control*, edited by Jalna Hamner and Mary Maynard, 169–79. London: Macmillan.

Drewry, Gavin, and Jenny Brock. 1983. *The Impact of Women on the House of Lords.* Glasgow: CSPP.

Dunleavy, Patrick, and Christopher Hasbands. 1985. *British Democracy at the Crossroads.* London: Allen and Unwin.

Edgell, Stephen, and Vic Duke. 1983. "Gender and Social Policy: The Impact of Public Expenditure Cuts and Reactions to Them." *Journal of Social Policy* 12:357–78.

Eduards, Maud. 1981. "Sweden." In *The Politics of the Second Electorate*, edited by Jill Hills and Joni Lovenduski, 208–28. London: Routledge and Kegan Paul.

———. 1986. "The Participation of Women in the Political Process in Sweden." Swedish Report to the Council of Europe. March.

Eduards, Maud, Beatrice Halsaa, and Hege Skjeie. 1985. "Equality: How Equal?" In *Unfinished Democracy: Women in Nordic Politics*, edited by Elina Haavio-Mannila et al., 131–59. Elmsford, N.Y.: Pergamon Press.

Elder, Neil, Alastair Thomas, and David Arter. 1982. *The Con-*

sensual Democracies? Government and Politics of the Scandinavian States. Oxford: Martin Robertson.

Elliott, Ruth. 1984. "How Far Have We Come? Women's Organizations and the Unions in the U.K." *Feminist Review* 16 (Summer 1984), 64–73.

Ellis, Valerie. 1981. "The Role of Trade Unions in the Promotion of Equal Opportunities." Manchester: Research Review Committee, EOC/SSRC Joint Panel on Equal Opportunities. August.

"Equality Between Men and Women in Sweden." 1987. *Fact Sheets on Sweden.* Stockholm: Swedish Institute. May.

Equality Ministry. 1985. *Side by Side: A Report on Equality Between Women and Men in Sweden, 1985.* Stockholm: Gotad.

Equal Opportunities Commission (EOC). 1981. *Grants for Equality, Research and Educational Activities Funded by the EOC, 1976–81.*

———. 1981. *Sixth Annual Report.* Manchester.

———. 1983. *Eighth Annual Report.* Manchester.

———. 1983–84. "Work and the Family." *Research Bulletin* no. 8, 37–48. Manchester.

———. 1987. "News Release." March 25, 1–2.

Erickson, Robert, and Rune Aberg. 1987. "The Nature and Distribution of Welfare." In *Welfare in Transition: A Study of Living Conditions, 1968–81,* edited by Robert Erickson and Rune Aberg, 1–14. Oxford: Clarendon Press.

Euro-Barometer 19: Gender Roles in the European Community. 1983. Ann Arbor: Interuniversity Consortium for Political and Social Research, University of Michigan.

Evans, Richard. 1977. *The Feminists.* London: Croom Helm.

Feminist Anthology Collective. 1981. *No Turning Back.* London: Women's Press.

Ferguson, Thomas, and Joel Rogers. 1986. "The Myth of America's Turn to the Right." *Atlantic,* May 43–49.

Flammang, Janet. 1984. "Filling the Party Vacuum: Women at the Grassroots Level in Local Politics." In *Political Women,* edited by Janet Flammang, 87–114. Beverly Hills, Calif.: Sage.

Flannery, Kate, and Sara Roelofs. 1984. "Local Government Women's Committees." In *Feminist Action I,* edited by Joy

Holland, 69–90. London: Battle Axe Books.

Fleming, Jane. 1983. "Wider Opportunities for Women: The Search for Equal Employment." In *Women in Washington*, edited by Irene Tinker, 78–89. Beverly Hills, Calif.: Sage.

Freeman, Jo. 1975. *The Politics of Women's Liberation*. New York: McKay.

———. 1985. "The Women's Movement and the 1984 Republican and Democratic Conventions." Manuscript.

———. 1985–86. "The Political Culture of the Democratic and Republican Parties." *Political Science Quarterly* 101 (3): 327–56.

———. 1987. "Whom You Know vs. Whom You Represent: Feminist Influence in the Democratic and Republican Parties." In *The Women's Movements of the United States and Western Europe*, edited by Mary Katzenstein and Carol Mueller, 215–46. Philadelphia: Temple University Press.

Gelb, Joyce. 1983. "The Politics of Wife Abuse." In *Families, Politics, and Public Policy*, edited by Irene Diamond, 250–62. New York: Longman.

Gelb, Joyce, and Ethel Klein. 1983. *Women's Movements: Organizing for Change in the 1980's*. Washington, D.C.: American Political Science Association.

Gelb, Joyce, and Marian Palley. 1987. *Women and Public Policies*. 2d ed. Princeton: Princeton University Press.

Gelb, Norman. 1983. "Britain's New Ruling Class." *New Leader*, June 27:8–9.

Gerlach, Luther, and Virginia Hine. 1970. *People, Power, Change: Movements of Social Transformation*. Indianapolis: Bobbs-Merrill.

Glucklich, Pauline. 1984. "The Effect of Statutory Employment Policies on Women in the U.K. Labour Market." In *Sex Discrimination and Equal Opportunity*, edited by Gunther Schmid and Renate Weitzel, 107–31. New York: St. Martin's Press.

Gold, Carol. 1977. "Two Routes Toward the Same Place." *Scandinavian Review* 65 (September): 10–12.

Golding, Peter, and Sue Middleton. 1982. *Images of Welfare: Press and Public Attitudes*. London: Martin Robertson.

Goodin, Joan M. 1983. "Working Women: The Pros and Cons

of Unions." In *Women in Washington*, edited by Irene Tinker, 140–47. Beverly Hills, Calif.: Sage.

Gordon, Diana, et al. 1982. *Seizing Our Opportunities: A Woman's Guide to Public Life*. London: European Union of Women.

Goss, Sue. 1984. "Women's Initiatives in Local Government." In *Local Socialism*, edited by D. Boddy and C. Fudge, 109–32. London: Macmillan.

Grant, Jane. 1988. *Sisters Across the Atlantic*. London: National Council for Voluntary Organizations.

Grant, Wyn. 1984. "The Role and Power of Pressure Groups." In *British Politics in Perspective*, edited by R. L. Borthwick and S. C. Spence, 123–45. New York: St. Martin's Press.

Greenburger, Marcia. 1980. "The Effectiveness of Federal Laws Prohibiting Sex Discrimination in Employment in the U.S." In *Equal Employment Policy for Women*, edited by Ronnie Steinberg Ratner, 108–27. Philadelphia: Temple University Press.

Greenwood, Karen, and Lucy King. 1981. "Contraception and Abortion." In *Women in Society: Interdisciplinary Essays*, edited by Cambridge Women's Studies Group, 168–84. London: Virago.

Gustafsson, Siv. 1984. "Equal Opportunities Policies in Sweden." In *Sex Discrimination and Equal Opportunity*, edited by Gunther Schmid and Renate Weitzel, 132–54. New York: St. Martin's Press.

Haavio-Mannila, Elina, et al., eds. 1985. *Unfinished Democracy: Women in Nordic Politics*. Elmsford, N.Y.: Pergamon Press.

Hagtvet, Bernt, and Erik Buding. 1986. "Scandinavia: Achievements, Dilemmas, Challenges." In *Norden: The Passion for Equality*, edited by Stephen Graubard, 280–302. Oslo: Norwegian Universities Press.

Handler, Joel. 1978. *Social Movements and the Legal System*. New York: Academic Press.

Hanmer, Julia. 1977. "Community Action, Women's Aid and the Women's Liberation Movement." In *Women in the Com-*

munity, edited by Marjorie Mayo, 91–108. London: Routledge and Kegan Paul.

Harrison, Cynthia. 1984. "Politics and Law." In *Women's Annual: 1983–84*, edited by Sarah M. Prichard, 145–66. Boston: G. Hall.

Hastings, Elizabeth, and Philip K. Hastings, eds. 1982. *Index to International Public Opinion: 1980 to 1981*. Westport, Conn.: Greenwood Press.

———. 1983. *Index to International Public Opinion: 1981 to 1982*. Westport, Conn.: Greenwood Press.

———. 1985. *Index to International Public Opinion: 1983 to 1984*. Westport, Conn.: Greenwood Press.

———. 1986. *Index to International Public Opinion: 1984 to 1985*. Westport, Conn.: Greenwood Press.

———. 1987. *Index to International Public Opinion, 1985 to 1986*. Westport, Conn.: Greenwood Press.

Heckscher, Gunnar. 1984. *The Welfare State and Beyond*. Minneapolis: University of Minnesota Press.

Heclo, Hugh. 1974. *Modern Social Policies in Britain and Sweden*. New Haven: Yale University Press.

———. 1980. "The Executive Establishment." In *The New American Political System*, edited by Anthony King, 87–124. Washington, D.C.: American Enterprise Institute.

Heclo, Hugh, and Henrik Madsen. 1987. *Policy and Politics in Sweden: Principled Pragmatism*. Philadelphia: Temple University Press.

Hedlund, Gun, and Jaaneke van der Ros Schive. 1984. "The Impact of the Women's Liberation Movement on Local Politics: Experiences from Norway and Sweden." Paper presented to the IPSA Research Committee on Sex Roles and Politics at the Round Table, Sofia, October.

Heidenheimer, Arnold, Hugh Heclo, and Carolyn Adams. 1983. *Comparative Public Policy: The Politics of Social Choice in Europe and America*. 2d ed. New York: St. Martin's Press.

Hernes, Helga. 1982. "The Role of Women in Voluntary Associations." Part III of preliminary study submitted to the

Steering Committee of Human Rights (CDDH), Council of
Europe.
————. 1983. "Women and the Welfare State: The Transition
from Private to Public Dependence." Paper presented at
conference on "The Transformation of the Welfare State:
Dangers and Potentialities for Women," Bellagio, Italy,
August.
————. 1984. "Women and the Welfare State: The Transition
from Private to Public Dependence." In *Patriarchy in a Wel-
fare Society*, edited by Harriet Holter, 26–46. Oslo: Universi-
tetsforlaget.
Hernes, Helga, and Eva Hanninen-Salmelin. 1985. "Women in
the Corporate System." In *Unfinished Democracy: Women in
Nordic Politics*, edited by Elina Haavio-Mannila et al., 106–
33. Elmsford, N.Y.: Pergamon Press.
Heron, Sylvie. 1983. "The Other Face of Feminism." *New
Statesman*, April 11–13.
Hewlett, Sylvia Ann. 1986. *A Lesser Life: The Myth of Women's
Liberation in America.* New York: Morrow.
Hills, Jill. 1978. "Women in the Labour and Conservative Par-
ties." Paper presented at the Annual Conference of the Po-
litical Science Association, Warwick, England.
————. 1981. "Britain." In *Politics of the Second Electorate*,
edited by Jill Hills and Joni Lovenduski, 8–32. London:
Routledge and Kegan Paul.
Holland, Joy, ed. 1984. *Feminist Action I.* London: Battle Axe
Books.
Holmberg, Soren. 1986. "Gender/Party vs. Questions Dealing
with Women in Sweden, 1976–85." SAS Institute, Univer-
sity of Gothenburg, Göteborgs Central. June.
Hunt, Judith. 1982. "A Woman's Place Is in Her Union." In
Work, Women, and the Labour Market, edited by Jackie
West, 154–71. London: Routledge and Kegan Paul.
Hoskyns, Catherine. "Women's Equality and the European
Community." *Feminist Review* 20 (Summer): 71–90.
Huws, Ursula. 1985. "Women and Employment." In *The In-
visible Decade: U.K. Women in the United Nations, Decade*

1976–1985, edited by Georgina Ashworth and Lucy Bonnerjea, 50–62. Aldershot, Hants: Gower.

Hyman, Colette A. 1985. "Labor Organizing and Female Institution Building: The Chicago Women's Trade Union League, 1904–24." In *Women, Work and Protest*, edited by Ruth Milkman, 22–42. Boston: Routledge and Kegan Paul.

Inglehart, Ronald. 1977. *The Silent Revolution*. Princeton: Princeton University Press.

International Gallup Poll. 1981. London: George Prior Association.

International Labour Office Staff. 1985. *Year Book of Labour Statistics, 1984*. 44th ed. Geneva: ILO.

Jackson, Christine. 1984. "Policies and Implementation of Anti-discrimination Strategies." In *Sex Discrimination and Equal Opportunity*, edited by Gunther Schmid and Renate Weitzel, 191–201. New York: St. Martin's Press.

Jacobson, Gary. 1985. "Congress: Politics After a Landslide Without Coattails." In *The Election of 1984*, edited by Michael Nelson, 215–38. Washington, D.C.: Congressional Quarterly Press.

JA SAF/PTK. 1987. *Siffror om Män och Kvinnor.* Stockholm.

Jenkins, Craig. 1983. "Resource Mobilization Theory and the Study of Social Movements." In *Annual Review of Sociology*, 527–53. Palo Alto, Calif.: Annual Reviews.

Jenson, Jane. 1982. "The Modern Women's Movement in Italy, France and Great Britain: Differences in Life Cycles." In *Comparative Social Research: Annual*, 341–75. Greenwich, Conn.: JAI Press.

———. 1983. "Success Without Struggle? The Modern Women's Movement in France." Paper presented at the Cornell University Workshop on the Women's Movement in Comparative Perspective, May 6–8.

Jones, Meg. 1984. *Thatcher's Kingdom*. Sydney: Collins.

Jonung, Christine. 1984. "Patterns of Occupational Segregation by Sex in the Labour Market." In *Sex Discrimination and Equal Opportunity*, edited by Gunther Schmid and Renate Weitzel, 44–68. New York: St. Martin's Press.

Jonung, Christina, and Bodil Thordarsson. 1980. "Sweden." In *Women Returning to Work: Policies and Progress in Five Countries*, edited by Alice Yohalem, 107–59. Montclair, N.J.: Allanheld, Osmun.

Judge, Ken, Jillian Smith, and Peter Taylor Gooby. 1983. "Public Opinion and the Privatization of Welfare." *Journal of Social Policy* 12 : 469–90.

Kamerman, Sheila. 1984. "Women, Children and Poverty: Public Policies and Female Headed Families in Industrialized Countries." *Signs* 10(2): 249–71.

Kamerman, Sheila, Alfred Kahn, and Paul Kingston. 1983. *Maternity Policies for Working Women*. New York: Columbia University Press.

Kelman, Steven. 1981. *Regulating America/Regulating Sweden*. Cambridge: MIT Press.

———. 1984. "Party Strength and Governability in the Face of New Political Demands: The Case of Feminism." J. F. Kennedy School of Government, Cambridge, Massachusetts. Typescript.

Kesselman, Mark, and Joel Krieger. 1987. *European Politics in Transition*. Lexington, Mass.: Heath.

Kessler-Harris, Alice. 1985. "Problems of Coalition Building: Women and Trade Unions in the 1920's." In *Women, Work and Protest*, edited by Ruth Milkman, 110–38. Boston: Routledge and Kegan Paul.

Kingdom, Elizabeth. 1985. "Legal Recognition of a Woman's Right to Choose." In *Women in Law*, edited by Julia Brophy and Carol Smart, 143–61. London: Routledge and Kegan Paul.

Kolker, Ann. 1983. "Women Lobbyists." In *Women in Washington*, edited by Irene Tinker, 209–222. Beverly Hills, Calif.: Sage.

Land, Hilary. 1983. "Who Still Cares for the Family? Recent Developments in Income Maintenance, Taxation and Family Law." In *Women's Welfare/Women's Rights*, edited by Jane Lewis, 64–88. London: Croom Helm.

Landsorganisationen (LO). 1984. *Kvinnor i Facket* [Women in Trade Unions]. Stockholm.

Langford, C. M. "Attitudes of British Women to Abortion: Trends." *Population Trends* 22 : 11 – 13.

Law, Sylvia. 1988. "Girls Can't Be Plumbers": Affirmative Action in Construction—Beyond Goals and Quotas. Draft paper. New York University School of Law.

Levine, David. 1986. "Political Economy: Mapping the Terrain." Department of Economics, University of Denver. Typescript.

Lewis, Jane. 1983. "Introduction" and "Dealing with Dependency: State Practices and Social Realities." In *Women's Welfare/Women's Rights,* edited by Jane Lewis, 1–7 and 17–37. London: Croom Helm.

———. "Work, Women and Welfare." In *The Future of Welfare,* edited by Rudolph Klein and Michael O'Higgins, 216–21. Oxford: Basil Blackwell.

Light, Paul, and Celinda Lake. 1985. "The Election: Candidates' Strategies and Decisions." In *The Election of 1984,* edited by Michael Nelson, 83–110. Washington: Congressional Quarterly Press.

Livingston, Kenneth (interview). 1984. "Local Socialism: The Way Ahead." In *Local Socialism,* edited by D. Boddy and C. Fudge, 242–84. London: Macmillan.

Lorwin, Val, and Sara Boston. 1984. "Great Britain." In *Women and Trade Unions in Eleven Industrialized Countries,* edited by Alice Cook, 140–61. Philadelphia: Temple University Press.

Lovenduski, Joni. 1986. *Women and European Politics: Contemporary Feminism and Public Policy.* Amherst: University of Massachusetts Press.

Lowi, Theodore. 1971. *The Politics of Disorder.* New York: Free Press.

Lundqvist, Lennart. 1980. *The Hare and the Tortoise: Clean Air Policy in the United States and Sweden.* Ann Arbor: University of Michigan Press.

McCann, Katherine. 1985. "Battered Women and the Law: The Limits of Legislation." In *Women in Law,* edited by Julia Brophy and Carol Smart, 71–96. London: Routledge and Kegan Paul.

MacCann, Michael. 1986. *Taking Reform Seriously: Perspectives on Public Interest Liberalism.* Ithaca: Cornell University Press.

McCarthy, J. J., and Meyer Zald. 1975. *The Trend of Social Movements in America: Professionalization and Resource Mobilization.* Morristown, N.J.: General Learning Press.

———. 1977. "Resources Mobilization and Social Movements: A Partial Theory." *American Journal of Sociology* 82: 1212–42.

McFarland, Andrew. 1984. *Common Cause.* Chatham, N.J.: Chatham House.

Mailler, A. T., and M. J. Rosser. 1987. *Women and the Economy.* New York: St. Martin's Press.

Mandel, Ruth. 1982. *In the Running: The New Woman Candidate.* New York: Ticknor and Fields.

Mansbridge, Jane. 1980. *Beyond Adversary Democracy.* New York: Basic Books.

Market and Opinion Research International (MORI). 1978–84. (Various polls.) London.

Marsh, David, and Joanna Chambers. 1981. *Abortion Politics.* London: Junction Books.

———. 1983a. "Equal Opportunities Policies: Some Implications for Women of Contrasts Between Enforcement Bodies in Britain and the U.S.A." In *Women's Welfare/Women's Rights,* edited by Jane Lewis, 170–91. London: Croom Helm.

———. 1983b. "The Priorities of EOC." *Political Quarterly* 54 (January–March): 69–86.

———. 1985. *Women's Rights at Work.* New York: St. Martin's Press.

Mellstrom, Gunilla Furst, and Marian Sterner. 1980. "Improved Working Conditions and Advancement Opportunities of Women (The State Administration Taken as an Example: A Comparative Study in the U.S.A., Sweden and the FRG)." Department of Sociology, University of Gothenburg, Fredrich Ebert Stiftung. Typescript.

Milkman, Ruth. 1985. "Women Workers, Feminism and the Labour Movement Since the 1960's." In *Women, Work and*

Protest, edited by Ruth Milkman, 300–322. Boston: Routledge and Kegan Paul.

Morgan, Robin, ed. 1984. *Sisterhood Is Global: The International Women's Movement Anthology.* Garden City, N.Y.: Anchor Press/Doubleday.

Mueller, Carol. 1983. "Women's Movement Success and the Success of Social Movement Theory." Working Paper no. 710. Center for Research on Women, Wellesley College.

National Council for Voluntary Organizations (NCVO). 1981. "The Voluntary Sector." Information Sheet 6, no. 3. London. April.

Nelkin, Dorothy, and Michael Pollak. 1981. *The Atom Besieged: Extraparliamentary Dissent in France and West Germany.* Cambridge: MIT Press.

Norris, Pippa. 1984. "Women in Poverty: Britain and America." *Journal of Social Policy* 13 : 22–44.

———. [1986] "Women in Congress: A Policy Difference?" *Politics* 6, no. 1 : 34–40.

———. 1988. "The Gender Gap: A Cross National Trend?" In *The Politics of the Gender Gap*, edited by Carol M. Mueller, 217–34. Beverly Hills, Calif.: Sage.

Oakley, Ann. 1983. "Women and Health Policy." In *Women's Welfare/Women's Rights*, edited by Jane Lewis, 103–29. London: Croom Helm.

Olsen, M. 1982. *Participatory Pluralism.* Chicago: Nelson Hall.

Parkin, Frank. 1968. *Middle Class Radicalism.* Manchester: Manchester University Press.

Pennock, J. Roland, and John W. Chapman, eds. 1969. *Voluntary Associations.* New York: Lieber-Atherton.

Perrigo, Sarah. 1985. "The Women's Movement Patterns of Resistance and Oppression." In *A Socialist Anatomy of Britain*, edited by David Coates, Gordon Johnston, and Ray Bush, 124–45. Cambridge: Polity Press.

Peterson, Abby. 1984. "The Gender/Sex Dimension in Swedish Politics." *Acta Sociologia* 27 (1): 3–17.

Peterson, Esther. 1983. "The Kennedy Commission." In *Women in Washington*, edited by Irene Tinker, 213–15. Beverly Hills, Calif.: Sage.

Peterson, Mark, and Jack Walker. 1986. "Interest Group Responses to Partisan Changes: The Impact of the Reagan Administration upon the National Interest Group System." In *Interest Group Politics*, edited by Allen J. Cigler and Burton Loomis, 162–82. Washington, D.C.: Congressional Quarterly Press.

Phillips, Andrew. 1982. *Charitable Status*. London: Interaction.

Phillips, Anne. 1983. *Hidden Hands*. London: Pluto Press.

Pierce, Sylvia. 1980. "Single Mothers and the Concept of Female Dependency in the Development of the Welfare State in Britain." *Journal of Comparative Family Studies* 11 (Winter): 57–85.

Pleck, Elizabeth. 1987. *Domestic Tyranny: The Making of American Social Policy Against Family Violence*. Oxford: Clarendon Press.

Poole, Keith T., and Harmon L. Zeigler. 1985. *Women, Public Opinion and Politics*. New York: Longman.

Popenoe, David. 1985–86. "Beyond Tradition: A Statistical Portrait of the Changing Swedish Family." Rutgers University. Typescript.

Punnett, R. M. 1980. *British Government and Politics*. London: Heineman.

Pym, Bridget. 1974. *Pressure Groups and the Permissive Society*. Newton Abbott: David and Clarks.

Qvist, Gunnar, Joan Acker, and Val R. Lorwin. 1984. "Sweden." In *Women and Trade Unions in Eleven Industrialized Countries*, edited by Alice Cook et al., 261–85. Philadelphia: Temple University Press.

Randall, Vicky. 1982. *Women and Politics*. New York: St. Martin's Press.

Rasmussen, Jorgen. 1983a. "Political Integration of British Women." *Social Science History* 4 (Winter): 61–95.

———. 1983b. "Women's Role in Contemporary British Politics: Impediments to Parliamentary Candidature." *Parliamentary Affairs* 36(3): 300–315.

Ratner, Ronnie Steinberg, ed. 1980. *Equal Employment Policy for Women*. Philadelphia: Temple University Press.

Rein, Martin. 1985. "Women, Employment, and Social Welfare." In *The Future of Social Welfare,* edited by Rudolf Klein and Michael O'Higgins, 37–58. Oxford: Basil Blackwell.

Rendel, Margherita. 1978. "Legislating for Equal Pay and Opportunity in Britain." *Signs* 3:897–908.

Richardson, J. T., and A. G. Jordan. 1979. *Governing Under Pressure.* London: Martin Robertson.

Rivers, Patrick. 1974. *Politics Under Pressure.* London: Merlin Press.

Robarts, Sadye, Anna Coate, and E. Ball. 1980. *Positive Action for Women.* London: National Council for Civil Liberties.

Robertson, David. 1984. "Adversary Politics, Public Opinion and Electoral Cleavages." In *Essays in Honor of S. E. Finer,* edited by D. Kavanaugh and Gillian Peele, 30–45. London: Heineman.

Robinson, Pamela. 1982. *Women's Action Group Committee Report.* London: Women's Action Group. July.

Rogers, Barbara. 1983. *52%—Getting Women's Power into Politics.* London: Women's Press.

Roos, Patricia. 1985. *Gender and Work: A Comparative Analysis of Industrial Societies.* Albany: State University of New York Press.

Roper Organization. 1980. "Virginia Slims 1980 Public Opinion Poll." New York.

Rose, Richard. 1986. *Politics in England.* Boston: Little, Brown.

Rothwell, Sheila. 1980. "United Kingdom." In *Women Returning to Work: Politics and Progress in Five Countries,* edited by Alice Yohalem, 160–216. Montclair, N.J.: Allanheld, Osmun.

Rowbotham, Sheila. 1979. *Beyond the Fragments.* London: Merlin Press.

———. 1983. *Dreams and Dilemmas.* London: Virago.

———. 1984. "Sharing the Caring." *New Statesman,* June 13, 8–10.

Ruggie, Mary. 1984. *The State and Working Women.* Princeton: Princeton University Press.

———. 1986. "Gender, Worker and Social Progress: Some Consequences of Interest Aggregation in Sweden." Paper presented at the Conference on "Work and Politics: The Feminization of the Labor Force," Center for European Studies, Harvard University, March 14–16.

Sainsbury, Diane. 1983. "Who Participates in Scandinavian Politics? An Explanatory Overview of Patterns of Political Participation in Denmark, Norway and Sweden." Paper presented at the Sixth Annual Meeting of the International Society of Political Psychology. St. Catherine's College, Oxford, July 19–22.

————. 1985. "Women's Routes to National Legislatures: A Comparison of Eligibility and Nomination in the United States, Britain and Sweden." Paper presented at the Annual Meeting of the Swedish Political Science Association, Stockholm, October 28–29.

Sampson, Anthony. 1982. *The Changing Anatomy of Britain.* New York: Random House.

Schechter, Susan. 1982. *Women and Male Violence.* Boston: South End Press.

Schmitter, Philippe C. 1984. "Still the Century of Corporatism?" *Review of Politics* 36 (January): 85–131.

Scott, Hilda. 1982. *Sweden's Right to Be Human.* London: Allison and Busby.

Sebestyen, Amanda. 1979. *Notes from the Tenth Year.* London: Theory Press.

Seifer, Nancy, and Barbara Wertheimer. 1979. "New Approaches to Collective Power: Four Working Women's Organizations." In *Women Organizing: An Anthology,* edited by Beatrice Cummings and Victoria S. Shuck, 152–83. Metuchen, N.J.: Scarecrow Press.

Seyd, Patrick. 1976. "The Child Poverty Action Group." *Political Studies* 47 : 189–202.

Siim, Berthe. 1985. "A Comparative Perspective on Women and the Welfare State." Paper presented at the Center for Research at Stanford University.

Sinkkonen, Sirkka. 1985. "Women in Local Politics." In *Unfinished Democracy: Women in Nordic Politics,* edited by Elina Haavio-Mannila et al., 81–105. Elmsford, N.Y.: Pergamon Press.

Sjoblom, Gunnar. 1986. "The Role of Political Parties in Denmark and Sweden." Institute of Political Studies, University of Copenhagen. Typescript.

Skard, Torild, and Elina Haavio-Mannila. 1985. "Women in Parliament" and "Mobilization of Women at Elections." In *Unfinished Democracy: Women in Nordic Politics,* edited by Elina Haavio-Mannila et al., 37–50 and 51–80. Elmsford, N.Y.: Pergamon Press.

Smith, B. C. 1976. *Policy Making in British Government.* London: Martin Robertson.

Smith, Roger. 1980. "Images and Equality: Women and the National Press." *Sociological Review Monograph* 29 (October): 239–58.

Social Welfare in Britain. 1987. London: Central Office of Information.

Speakman, Sue. 1984. "Women and Shiftwork: A Study of the Effects of Shiftworking Patterns on Work Opportunities and Family Life." *EOC Research Bulletin* 8:37–48.

Stacey, Margaret, and Marion Price. 1980. *Women, Power and Politics.* London: Tavistock.

Statistical Abstract of Sweden, 1987. 1987. Stockholm: Central Bureau of Statistics.

Stott, Mary. 1978. *Organization Women.* London: Heineman.

Sundstrom, Marianne. 1985. "A Study in the Growth of Part-Time Work in Sweden." Arbetslivcentrum, Stockholm. Preliminary draft.

Szulkin, Ryszard. 1987. "Political Resources." In *Welfare in Transition: A Study of Living Conditions, 1968–81,* edited by Robert Erickson and Rune Aberg, 194–216. Oxford: Clarendon Press.

Tahlin, Michael. 1987. "Leisure and Recreation." In *Welfare in Transition: A Study of Living Conditions, 1968–81,* edited by Robert Erickson and Rune Aberg, 234–59. Oxford: Clarendon Press.

Tarrow, Sidney. 1983. *Struggling to Reform: Social Movements and Policy Change During Cycles of Protest.* Occasional Paper no. 15. Western Societies Program, Center for International Studies, Cornell University.

Temkin, Jennifer. 1986. "Women, Rape and Law Reform." In *Rape*, edited by Sylvana Tomaselli and Roy Porter, 17–40. Oxford: Basil Blackwell.

Thompson, Joan Hulse. 1984. "The Congressional Caucus for Women's Issues: One Hundred and Thirty Feminists in the House." Paper presented at the Midwest Political Science Association meeting, Chicago, April 11–14.

Tinker, Irene. 1983. "Two Decades of Insurance." In *Women in Washington*, edited by Irene Tinker, 9–16. Beverly Hills, Calif.: Sage.

Tomes, Hilary. 1985. "Women and Education." In *The Invisible Decade: U.K. Women in the United Nations, Decade 1976–1985*, edited by Georgina Ashworth and Lucy Bonnerjea, 32–45. Aldershot, Hants: Gower.

Trades Union Conference. 1982. *Women's Conference Report.* London: Trades Union Congress.

Trades Union Congress (TUC). 1982. "Report for 1981–1982 for the Women's Advisory Committee." London. March.

Transport and General Workers Union (TGWU). 1980. "Women's Handbook: Policies and Action." London.

UNESCO. 1983. "General Introduction." *Bibliographic Guide to Studies on the Status of Women*, 24–31. Paris.

Vallance, Elizabeth. 1979. *Women in the House.* London: Athlone Press.

———. 1984. "Women Candidates in the 1983 General Election." *Parliamentary Affairs* 37(3): 301–9.

———. 1985. "Equality and the Formation of Public Policy." In *The Invisible Decade: U.K. Women in the United Nations, Decade 1976–1985*, edited by Georgina Ashworth and Lucy Bonnerjea, 20–32. Aldershot, Hants: Gower.

Van der Gaag, Virginia. 1985. "Women Organizing." In *The Invisible Decade: U.K. Women in the United Nations, Decade 1976–1985*, edited by Georgina Ashworth and Lucy Bonnerjea, 133–40. Aldershot, Hants: Gower.

Verba, Sidney, and Gary Orren. 1985. *Equality in America: The View from the Top.* Cambridge: Harvard University Press.

Walker, Jack. 1983. "The Origins and Maintenance of Interest Groups in America." *American Political Science Review* 77 (June): 390–406.

Wandor, Michelle. 1972. *Body Politic*. London: Stage One.

Weir, Angel, and Elizabeth Wilson. 1984. "The British Women's Movement." *New Left Review* 48 (November–December): 74–103.

Wertheimer. 1984. "The U.S.A." In *Women and Trade Unions*, edited by Alice Cook et al., 286–311. Philadelphia: Temple University Press.

Whitely, Paul, and Steven Winyard. 1983. "Influencing Social Policy: The Effectiveness of the Poverty Lobby in Britain." *Journal of Social Policy* 12:10–11.

Williscroft, Sue. 1985. "Women and the Law." In *The Invisible Decade: U.K. Women in the United Nations, Decade 1976–1985*, edited by Georgina Ashworth and Lucy Bonnerjea, 97–107. Aldershot, Hants: Gower.

Wilson, Elizabeth. 1980. *Only Half Way to Paradise*. London: Tavistock.

Wistrand, Birgitta. 1982. *Swedish Women on the Move*. Stockholm: Swedish Institute.

Women and Men in Sweden: Facts and Figures. 1985. Stockholm: Statistics Sweden.

"Women's Equality and the European Community." *Feminist Review*, no. 20 (Summer): 70–88.

Women's National Commission (WNC). 1982. "Background Note." January.

Wormald, Eileen, and Ivan Reid. 1982. *Sex Differences in Britain*. London: Groot McIntyre.

Yohalem, Alice, ed. 1980. *Women Returning to Work: Politics and Progress in Five Countries*. Montclair, N.J.: Allanheld, Osmun.

Zald, Mayer, and Roberta Ash. 1966. "Social Movement Organizations." *Social Forces* 44: 327–41.

Zeitlin, June. 1983. "Domestic Violence: Perspectives from Washington." In *Women in Washington*, edited by Irene Tinker, 263–75. Beverly Hills, Calif.: Sage.

Newspapers and Journals

Chronicle of Higher Education. 1986.
Economist. 1982–87.
Employment Gazette. 1984.
Equal Opportunities Commission News. 1981–82.
Guardian. 1979–87.
Money. 1986.
Ms. 1984–86.
Nation. 1983.
New Statesman. 1980–86.
Newsweek. 1981–86.
New York Times. 1979–87.
Population Trends. 1980–87.
Spare Rib. 1981–85.
Women at Work. 1979–87. Geneva.
Women in Management Review. 1985–88.
Women's Fightback. 1982.

Interviews

United Kingdom (Individuals and Groups), 1980–84

Abdela, Lesley; 300 Group
Ashworth, Georgina; CHANGE
Barrett, Michelle
Brown, Sandra; Channel Four; EOC
Chambers, Joanna; Birth Control Trust
Campbell, Beatrix
Child Poverty Action Group (CPAG)
Coote, Anna; *New Statesman*
Davin, Anna
Davis, Kath; Scottish Convention of Women (SCOW)
Derer, Vera; WAG
Evans, Judi; St. Mary's College, University of London
Evans, Mary; University of Kent
Federation of Liberal Women
Gardner, Baroness Trixie

Gibson, Ann; NCCL; Women's Rights
Gould, Joyce; National Women's Officer, Labour Party
Henniker-Heaton, Lady Margaret; National Union of Towns-women's Guilds
Hewitt, Iffat; Anglo-Asian group, Conservative Party
Hogg, Mrs. Wendy M.; U.K. Federation of Business and Professional Women
Hooper, Angela; National Women's Officer, Conservative Party
Hunt, Judith; Tass; GLC
Lait, Jackie, Conservative Party
Lestor, Joan; M.P., Labour Party
Lever, Rachel; Fightback
Lockwood, Lady Betty; Chair, EOC
Longley, A. R.; Legal Advisor, National Council of Voluntary Organizations (NCVO)
Lovenduski, Joni; Loughborough University
MacDonald, Oonagh; M.P., Labour Party
McFarquar, Emily; *Economist*
Marsland, Terry; Tobacco Workers Union
Meehan, Elizabeth; University of Bath
Morrell, Frances; Labour Party
National Abortion Campaign (NAC)
National Women's Aid Federation (NWAF)
Organization of Women of African and Asian Descent (OWAAD)
Patterson, Marie; TGWU; TCU
Potter, Hilary; Women's Advisory Officer, Islington
Randall, Vicki; Central London Polytechnic
Rendel, Margherita; Institute of Education, University of London
Rights of Women (ROW)
Robinson, Pamela; Women in the Media; National Federation of Women's Institutes
Robarts, Sadye; NCCL
Sebestyen, Amanda
Seear, Baroness Nancy
Slipman, Sue; SDP
Social Democratic Party (SDP)

Spender, Dale
Stott, Mary; Fawcett Society; *Guardian*
Toynbee, Polly; *Guardian*
Trembath, Di; Public Information, EOC
Tuomin, Ann; National Secretary, WNC
Turner, Pat; National Women's Officer, GMWU
Vallance, Elizabeth; St. Mary's College
Williams, Shirley; M.P., (then) Labour Party; (now) SDP
Wingfield, Margaret; NCW
Wise, Valerie; Chair, Women's Committee, GLC
Women in the Media
Women's Action Group (WAG)
Woodcraft, Tess; NALGO
Young, Baroness Janet Mary; Conservative Party

Sweden, 1986

Axelsson, Christina; Researcher, Swedish Institute for Social
    Research, University of Stockholm
Baude, Annika; Arbetslivcentrum
Boye, Marianne; Kvinnocentrum (Women's House)
Branting, Charlotte; Swedish Federation of Liberal Women;
    M.P., Riksdag
Carlsson, Boel; Equality Matters, LO
Dahlberg, Anita; City Hall, Stockholm (Stockholm Kommun)
Dahlgren, Anita; Department of Sociology, University of Lund
Eduards, Maud; Department of Political Science, University
    of Stockholm
Fredricksson, Ingrid
Haglund, Ann Katherine; Moderate Party; M.P., Riksdag
Hedlund, Gun; Department of Political Science, University of
    Orebro
Hirdman, Yvonne; Women and Power Project, Delegation for
    Research on Equality (JAMFO); SDP
Johansson, Ann Marie; National Institute for Civil Service,
    Training, and Development (SIPU)
Karlsson, Eva; JAMFO
Karlsson, Viola; VPK; M.P., Riksdag

Lidbeck, Ase; Ministry of Labor
Lindqvist, Lena; SACO/SR
Lonroth, Ani; *Svenska Dagbladet*
Mitchell, Diane; Arbetslivcentrum
Mrul, Birgitta; Department of Sociology, Uppsala University
Olafsson, Birgitta; President, Stockholm Division, Frederika
　Bremer League
Onfelt, Cecelia; National Organization for Women's Shelters
　(RUKS); All Women's House, Stockholm
Peanberg, Kerstin; National Federation of Social Democratic
　Women
Persson, Margarita; SDP; M.P., Riksdag
Pettersson, Anita; Ombudsman, TCO
Sainsbury, Diane; Department of Political Science, University
　of Stockholm
Sangregorio, Inga; Group 8
Soderstrom, Eliabeth; Association of Center Party Women
Wadstein, Margareta; Deputy Equal Opportunities Ombuds-
　man, JämO
Wallstein, Margit; SAF
Wistrand, Birgitta; Positive Sweden; former president, Fre-
　derika Bremer League

Index

Abortion, 39–40; in Britain, 11, 105, 115–18, 133; on demand, 12, 36, 116, 130; legislation, 13, 14, 39, 168–69, 182, 203; policy-making, 90, 118; for poor women, 66; reform, 115–18; state funds for, 11; in Sweden, 14, 152; views of British women on, 133. *See also* National Abortion Campaign (Great Britain); National Abortion Rights Action League (United States)

Abortion Act (Great Britain, 1967), 13, 39, 182, 203

Abortion Act (Sweden, 1976), 168–69

Abortion Law Reform Association (Great Britain), 40, 115, 117

Abortion rights, 39–40; in Britain, 57, 188; in United States, 13, 64, 107

Abused women. *See* Battered women; Domestic violence

Act on Equality Between Men and Women (Sweden, 1979), 165

Advisory Conciliation and Arbitration Service (Great Britain), 108, 112

Advocacy of women: American and British contrasted, 103–5; government-based, 98–103

Affirmative action, 101, 103, 205; factors aiding, 104

Age discrimination, 83

"Aims for Women at Work" (document of Trades Union Congress, Great Britain), 74

American Federation of State, County, and Municipal Employees, 77, 79

American feminist movement. *See* American women's liberation movement

American party system. *See* Political parties, American

American Postal Workers Union, 79

American Telephone and Telegraph (AT&T): and civil rights legislation, 101

American women's liberation movement, 189–91, 220; characteristics of, 46–51, 184–86; coalitions, 47, 51; funding, 24–25; and govern-

Moberg, Eva, 163
Moderate Party (Sweden), 153
Mondale, Walter, 66
Mother's Union (Great Britain), 44
Municipal councils, Swedish, 140
Municipal officials, women (United States), 99

National Abortion Campaign (Great Britain), 39–41, 117, 133, 182; and social feminists, 41; and union groups, 71
National Abortion Council (Great Britain), 43
National Abortion Rights Action League (United States), 39, 49, 66, 89
National Center on Child Abuse and Neglect (United States), 125
National Coalition against Domestic Violence (United States), 47, 49, 123, 124
National Council for Civil Liberties (Great Britain), 23, 42, 68, 94, 96, 109, 119; and union groups, 71
National Council of Women (Great Britain), 23, 43
National Education Association (United States), 77
National Federation of Business and Professional Womens Clubs (United States), 190
National Federation of Republican Women, 65
National Federation of Social Democratic Women (Sweden), 151–52
National Federation of Women Workers (Great Britain), 72

National Federation of Women's Institutes (Great Britain), 44
National Housewives Register (Great Britain), 37
National Labour Women's Advisory Committee (Great Britain), 55
National Organization for Women (United States), 34, 47, 48–51, 89; coalitions with other feminist groups, 49; equal representation in Democratic Party, 65; establishment of, 123; goals of, 31; growth, 189; membership, 50, 185; in 1984 presidential campaign, 66; recruitment of women for office, 63–64
National Organization for Women's Shelters (Sweden), 172
National Union of Education (Great Britain), 71
National Women's Aid Federation (Great Britain), 38, 118–19, 182; and campaigning, 40
National Women's Charter (Great Britain, 1982), 56
National Women's Committee (Great Britain), 56
National Women's Political Caucus (United States), 34, 63, 67, 89, 185, 190; equal representation in Democratic Party, 65; in 1980 political campaign, 66
Networking, 4, 22, 46, 51, 185; absence of in Britain, 95
New Left, 33–35
New Right, 124, 131–32, 135, 211; and future of feminism, 127–29; and grass-roots lobbying, 128; in 1980 and 1984 political campaigns, 129–30

Against Women (Great Britain), 182
Women in the Media (Great Britain), 37, 42, 109, 182
Women's Action Committee (Labour Party), 55, 74
Women's Action Day (Great Britain, 1980), 43
Women's Action Group (Great Britain), 43, 96
Women's Aid (anti-violence group, Great Britain), 37, 38, 120, 204; grants to, 96
Women's Aid Federation (Great Britain), 44
Women's Bureau (United States), 99–100
Women's Campaign Fund (United States), 67
Women's Conference (Labour Party), 55
Women's Equal Employment Group (Great Britain), 86
Women's Equity Action League (United States), 34, 49, 101, 185
Women's groups: multi-issue versus single issue, 50; structure of, table 2
Women's Health Information Center (Great Britain), 96
Women's Information, Reference, and Enquiry Service (Great Britain), 36

Women's Institutes (Great Britain), 23, 42
Women's liberation movements, 5, 30; favorable feeling toward, table 11; politics of, 22, 45, 52
Women's National Commission (Great Britain), 97–98
Women's Place (Great Britain), 87
Women's Reproductive Rights Group (Great Britain), 41
Women's Research and Resources Center (Great Britain), 36, 87, 96
Women's Therapy Center (Great Britain), 96
Women's Trade Union League (Great Britain), 72
Working-class women, 35, 87; hostility to unions, 75–76; and union membership, 69, 79
Working mothers, 9–10
Working wives, attitudes toward, 193–95
Working Women (white-collar group, United States), 83, 84, 89
Working Women's Charter (document of British Communist Party), 68, 74

Young, Janet, Baroness, 58